# Muay Thai Basics

## Introductory Thai Boxing Techniques

# Muay Thai Basics

## Introductory Thai Boxing Techniques

**Christoph Delp**

BLUE SNAKE BOOKS

Berkeley, California

Published by Blue Snake Books, an imprint of North Atlantic Books
Berkeley, California

Cover and book design by Brad Greene
Originally published by Pietsch Verlag, Stuttgart, Germany, 2005
Printed in the United States of America

*Muay Thai Basics: Introductory Thai Boxing Techniques* is sponsored and published by the Society for the Study of Native Arts and Sciences (dba North Atlantic Books), an educational nonprofit based in Berkeley, California, that collaborates with partners to develop cross-cultural perspectives, nurture holistic views of art, science, the humanities, and healing, and seed personal and global transformation by publishing work on the relationship of body, spirit, and nature.

---

North Atlantic Books' publications are available through most bookstores. For further information, call 800-733-3000 or visit our websites at www.northatlanticbooks.com and www.bluesnakebooks.com.

---

PLEASE NOTE: The creators and publishers of this book disclaim any liabilities for loss in connection with following any of the practices, exercises, and advice contained herein. To reduce the chance of injury or any other harm, the reader should consult a professional before undertaking this or any other martial arts, movement, meditative arts, health, or exercise program. The instructions and advice printed in this book are not in any way intended as a substitute for medical, mental, or emotional counseling with a licensed physician or healthcare provider.

ISBN-13: 978-1-58394-140-9

Library of Congress Cataloging-in-Publication Data

Delp, Christoph, 1974–
    Muay Thai basics : introductory Thai boxing techniques / by Christoph Delp.
        p. cm.
    Summary: "Focuses on the history and development of Muay Thai as well as providing step-by-step technique and training instructions"—Provided by publisher.
    Includes bibliographical references (p.   ).
    ISBN 1-58394-140-1 (pbk.)
    1. Muay Thai—Thailand.   I. Title.
GV1127.T45D453 2005
796.83'09593—dc22                                    2005024270

7  8  9  10  VERSA 22  21  20

North Atlantic Books is committed to the protection of our environment. We print on recycled paper whenever possible and partner with printers who strive to use environmentally responsible practices.

## Muay Thai

Muay Thai, also referred to as Thai boxing, is a centuries-old traditional martial art. At the present time, it is taught as a sport for fitness, competition, and self-defense.

Muay Thai training promotes the fitness components of power, stamina, agility, coordination, and speed. By continuous training, and following a moderate program, physical fitness can be achieved and maintained in the long run.

As a competitive sport Muay Thai thrills the audience with its hard and spectacular fights. The athletes attack each other for five rounds at the highest technical level. Daily fights demonstrate the efficiency of the techniques.

Muay Thai techniques can be readily adopted for self-defense. In Muay Thai the students learn both how to evade attacks and how to counter.

# Table of Contents

# Preface

I had been involved in full-contact sports for several years before I decided to travel to Thailand for training in 1995. I went to the Maha Sarakham province in northeast Thailand to learn Muay Thai. Master Decha accepted me in his camp and invited me to live with his family. Over a period of several months, I was in continuous contact and dialogue with my trainers Master Decha, Saknipon Pitakvarin, and Kenpet Luksilum, which provided me with the opportunity for an intensive study of Muay Thai. During that time, I developed the concept for my first book, *Muay Thai: Sport and Self-Defense.*

My enthusiasm for Muay Thai, and the affection of the Decha family and their friends, were the reason for my regular subsequent travels to Thailand for training. I maintain friendly ties with this gym to this very day. In the years following my initial training, I have revisited it on a number of occasions in addition to training in other gyms.

I was fortunate to be trained by the several-time champions Apideh Sit Hiran at the Fairtex Gym and Master Chalee at the Muay Thai Institute. Some biographical notes on these fighters follow. In these two camps I had other good trainers, such as Master Natchaphol, Master Noi, Master Gong, Jakid Fairtex, Kom Fairtex, and Paisitong Jorsambad.

At all the camps in Bangkok, in the provinces of Maha Sarakham, Buriram, and Chonburi, in Pattaya and Koh Samui, which I visited for training, I always enjoyed a warm welcome and respectful treatment. All my experiences with trainers and athletes at Thai gyms were positive. I am very grateful for the help and assistance given to me for the nine Muay Thai books I have published so far.

Author Christoph Delp in front of the Muay Thai Institute, Bangkok, 1999.

Muay Thai, a part of Thai culture, should be made accessible to the general public. Muay Thai has given me so much joy; through my books I would like to pass it on. I hope that all readers enjoy these books and that Muay Thai provides them with as much pleasure as it gives me. You will find further information on Muay Thai on the Internet at www.muaythaidvd.com and www.christophdelp.com.

A heartfelt thank you to all who have helped me in the preparation of this book, particularly my family, Master Decha, Oliver and Eckhard Glatow, Amnuay Kesbumrung, Nopphadol Viwatkamolwat, Peraphan Rungsikulpiphat, Songchai Ratanasuban, Colonel Somphob Srisiri, Menny Ossi, Thomas Letté, Daniel Gallus, Richard Delp, and the fighters shown in the photographs.

## Trainers

**Chitsanupong Nittayaros**. Master Decha. Born 1960, 145 professional fights, many fights as an amateur. He studied sports and graduated in sports and health. He trained many successful Thai fighters and taught in Australia, Greece, Japan, the Philippines, and Brunei.

**Chalee Khuntharee**. Master Chalee. Fighter name Pharuhatlek Sitchunthong, born 1961, 219 professional fights, five-time champion in three different weight divisions. He studied sports and graduated in sports and health. Master Chalee is internationally known as the former head trainer at the Muay Thai Institute, Bangkok.

**Narong Songmanee**. Apideh Sit Hiran. Born 1935, approximately 300 professional fights, seven-time champion, challenger in boxing for the WBA and WBC title. Apideh Sit Hiran is considered a living Muay Thai legend and, to many, he is the best fighter of all time. He has also been very successful as a trainer at the Fairtex Gym, Bangkok, and worked outside Thailand in the United States.

# Part I
# Background

**Chorake Fard Hang (Spinning Heel Kick). This technique can be delivered successfully only by experts in Muay Thai.**

■ Chapter 1

# Development

The Thai national sport Muay Thai, also known as Thai boxing, thrills spectators with spectacular techniques, toughness, and the morale of the athletes. The martial art is practiced daily in numerous Thai stadiums. In the meantime, the sport has also attracted a large following outside of Thailand.

Prior to the start of the contest, the boxers perform a dance-like ceremony that is accompanied by music, as is the entire fight itself. The music and the screams of the fans and gambling spectators create an extraordinary atmosphere. In five rounds the athletes attack each other at the highest technical level, completely exhausting themselves. The techniques are carried out with feet, shinbones, fists, elbows, and knees.

The effectiveness of this martial art is demonstrated by the repeated visits to Thailand of masters of many diverse types of martial arts, who are forced to throw in the towel at an early stage of the Muay Thai contest.

## Muay Thai: Martial Art and Sport

Muay Thai originated as a martial art that served the people of Siam (former name of Thailand) to defend themselves against invaders from neighboring countries. The Siam people fought their battles armed with swords, lances, and Muay Thai techniques. At the time, Muay Thai already showed its effectiveness, and the techniques can still be used for self-defense today.

Along with the further development of weaponry and their decisive influence on the success of war, the athletic aspect of Muay Thai gained in importance. Although sport events were organized in Siam centuries ago, the further development of the techniques for use in armed conflicts had been of greater importance than the

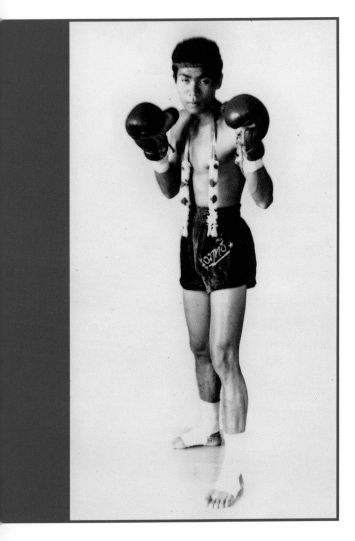

entertainment of an audience. The consequence was that rules and regulations for the events were standardized and stadiums were built in the 20th century.

Since the end of the 20th century more and more athletes have taken an interest in Muay Thai. By now, a large part of the public interested in sports is aware that Muay Thai is not only a means of self-defense, but also an excellent exercise to attain physical fitness.

Ajaarn Somboon Tapina prior to a fight, Thailand, 1960.

## Questions and Preconceptions

Thai boxers are repeatedly faced with prejudice toward and misunderstandings about their sport. This is probably due to insufficient information, but also to the improper use of the sport. Martial art trainers frequently mixed other components of their martial art with what they conceived to be typical Muay Thai elements and then offered a new course in their club. In addition, Thai and Asian trainers in neighboring countries saw this as a good opportunity to make money by teaching this fairly unknown type of martial art. However, it was not unusual for them to have no proper background in the sport, so that a particular type of training developed that appeared to be violent to many observers and that was apparently taught without rational explanation of the techniques. It was also noticed in Thailand that other types of martial arts had adopted an increasing number of Muay Thai elements. Thai boxing, however, did not enjoy a very positive reputation in the international community. Against this backdrop, the Thai government started to promote the real sport.

### ■ Are Muay Thai and Thai boxing identical?

Thai boxing is the internationally known name for Muay Thai. Muay Thai is the name of the sport in Thailand. Because of the questionable reputation attached to Thai boxing following the training methods of dubious teachers in some English-speaking regions, many supporters of the sport now prefer to call it Muay Thai.

The round kick misses its aim.

### ■ Did Muay Thai descend from kickboxing?

Kickboxing dates back to the 20th century. In contrast, Muay Thai is a centuries-old martial art. Kickboxing originated in two different regions: in North America, by changing the rules of Karate contests, and in Japan. A Japanese amended the rules of Muay Thai (for example, the use of elbows and knees was forbidden), began to open schools in Japan, and started to organize contests. This is one of the reasons for today's K1 tournaments with rules similar to those of Muay Thai, which are televised live from Japanese stadiums with audiences of more than 60,000.

Promoter Amnuay Kesbumrung.

### ■ What about tradition in Muay Thai?

Muay Thai is a centuries-old martial art, and many traditions developed in the course of time. One important tradition is the relationship between the teacher and the student.

Muay Thai offers athletic advantages over the untrained. It is the teacher's responsibility to ensure that his student treat the environment with respect and that he use Muay Thai, if so required, for the public good. A student who wishes to learn Muay Thai only in the interest of his athletic superiority should not be trained. Even long ago, Muay Thai teachers considered it their responsibility to educate their students in the tradition of respect for their fellow human beings.

It was and still is customary in Thailand for former students to pay a number of visits to their teachers in the course of their lives.

This includes old and inactive teachers, who are visited and given presents.

## Is Muay Thai an underground type of sport?

Many Thai boxers come from very poor social classes and try to improve the living conditions of their families with prize money. They leave school early. Some Thai managers exploit the situation and offer very poor living conditions in their gyms, and only successful boxers enjoy a reasonable existence. Some managers care little about the less fortunate fighters. That, however, is not the rule and the Thai government is taking steps to rectify the situation.

Bets are placed on all fights, and many spectators earn their living from the profits. Therefore, it is not a surprise that the results of fights are influenced as occurs in international boxing.

In some English-speaking regions, athletes frequently learned Muay Thai in order to test their newly acquired skills on the street. This was due to trainers who never studied the sport and never acquainted themselves with its tradition. For this reason they were unable to pass on important values of the sport to their students, such as respect for their fellow human beings.

However, the sport is becoming ever more popular. Many misunderstandings and preconceptions have been eliminated. Muay Thai has become a sport for the general public and is practiced by members of all social classes.

Joy after the bout for the title.

## What are the rules in Muay Thai?

Muay Thai is a strictly regulated sport. Generally, no techniques to the genitals, no head butts, and no attacks to the eyes are allowed.

A fighter falling down or lying on the floor may not be tackled. In female contests no elbows are permitted to the head.

### ■ Is Muay Thai fought with broken glass on the bandages?

At the present time, fights are conducted with boxing gloves. The question, whether in former times fights were carried out with broken glass attached to the bandages with wax, cannot be answered. However, it is assumed that sports contests were carried out with bandages, while warriors may, indeed, have attached sharp objects to the bandages.

### ■ Do athletes receive serious injuries during training and contests?

The risk of injury can never be completely excluded from a contact sport. Therefore, the training must be designed so that the athletes practice with each other and do not attempt to inflict any injuries.

In contrast to ball sports, such as soccer, the Muay Thai athletes can always see the opponent attacking. In contests between persons of a comparable athletic level the chance of injuries is rather low. However, there is a higher risk of injury in contests between athletes of different abilities, or in the case of insufficient preparation.

Due to the many techniques in Muay Thai, attacks to the opponent's head do not have the same significance as in traditional boxing. Consequently, Thai boxers are able to conduct a greater number of fights without grave injuries.

The former champions Niyom Ratanasit and Apideh Sit Hiran, both over 60 years of age and with records of more than 300 fights, confirm that they are still active in sports and are not suffering from any injuries. They are convinced that their Muay Thai training has strengthened their bodies and did not cause them any harm.

## Does Muay Thai training include tree kicking?

Some martial arts movies show Thai boxing being practiced on trees. At the present time, nobody practices this type of training. Centuries ago, in the absence of modern training equipment, the training method was applied to banana trees. These have been replaced by punching bags, whose contents vary in hardness in accordance with the stage of training.

Author, left, with Apideh Sit Hiran, one of the best fighters of all time.

## Who can learn Muay Thai?

The training is suited for both women and men. From an international viewpoint Muay Thai is registering the biggest growth in the number of female athletes. Even in Thailand contests between women are attracting continuously growing popularity.

One does not have to be an athlete to learn Muay Thai. In comparison to other types of martial arts less demands are made on agility on account of the many knee, fist, and elbow techniques. The training involves all groups of muscles, so that general physical fitness can be achieved. Due to the high intensity of training the sport is also exceptionally well suited for weight reduction.

Muay Thai is not restricted to a certain age. It can be taught to children and senior athletes alike. Ajaarn Somboon Tapina gave lessons to children in Australia. The children participated in large numbers and practiced with enthusiasm. Master Decha also reports of success with senior athletes in Australia.

In competition, however, rules usually apply relative to the age of contestants. Major health deficits—for example, in connection with vision and hearing—will prevent participation in athletic contests. A medical examination prior to a fight is compulsory, as are regular controls between contests.

### ■ Is it possible to learn Muay Thai properly only in Thailand?

If the trainer was comprehensively taught, the training can be at any location. At the present time, in the English-speaking regions, many teachers have an extensive background in Muay Thai. Some so-called trainers, however, offer their services on the basis of photos taken during visits to Thai camps. Thus, it is necessary to question the athletic competence of the potential trainer.

Time spent in Thailand, combined with a training program, significantly improves performance. It is recommended as an addition to the training at home. The book *Muay Thai: Advanced Thai Kickboxing Techniques* (Delp, 2004) gives an extensive account of training in Thailand and provides advice on what must be taken into consideration.

Training in Thailand to improve performance.

### ■ Can Muay Thai techniques be used effectively only by small individuals?

Frequently the opinion is voiced that Muay Thai is not suited for tall people. After all, goes the erroneous conclusion, the martial art was developed by the Thais, who are usually of a smaller size.

However, the large number of heavyweight fighters from many different nations who compete in K1 contests in Japan at a high athletic level show that Muay Thai can also be practiced successfully by tall athletes.

Athletes exceeding 7 feet in height also practice Muay Thai.

## History

The Thais originally lived in southwest China. In the ninth century the Thais migrated in groups to the area now known as northwest Thailand. The slow emigration lasted until the 13th century, and many conflicts with neighboring tribes occurred. During the wars weapons such as swords, lances, and knives were used. This particular type of martial art in combination with weapons is still being taught under the name Krabi Krabong. If the weapons were lost during the conflict, fighting continued with hand, elbow, and leg techniques. It is assumed that this was the beginning of Muay Thai and that it was continuously perfected in military training. Muay Thai was also taught in the provinces for protection of the local communities against robbers.

The Muay Boran technique
"Ramasul Kwang Kwoan."

The kingdom and the capital of the same name, Ayuthaya, were founded in 1350. The citizens were repeatedly faced with Burmese ambitions to occupy their land, which they were able to fend off successfully—also by the efficiency of the martial arts Krabi Krabong and Muay Thai—until 1569, when Ayuthaya was annexed as a Burmese province. After the Thai prince Narasuen defeated the Burmese successor to the throne in a duel in 1592, he drove the Burmese out of the country. A time of prosperity and peace followed. First contacts with the West were made. The Thai kings continued to be aware of the importance of Muay Thai and had intensive studies conducted at the royal residence. Many different types were compared and combined, in order to further improve the efficiency of Muay Thai. (At the present time, the techniques of these traditional styles are taught under the name of Muay Boran.)

During this time period the Thai King Pra Chao Sua (King Tiger) appreciated the martial art to the extent that he himself also practiced it intensively. To test his skills he traveled to village festivities in disguise and defeated the best athletes in competitive contests.

Ayuthaya, one of the most thriving towns in the East, was conquered by the Burmese in 1767 and burned down to the ground. Nearly all the official archives were lost, which is why many details of Thai history and the history of Muay Thai remain somewhat vague. Subsequently, the Burmese enslaved many Thais. According to legend the Burmese king asked the captured Thais at a ceremony in 1770 which Thai wanted to fight Burma. The Thai Nai Kha Nom Tom volunteered and defeated in succession the 10 best Burmese fighters. The Burmese granted him one wish, after which Nai Kha Nom Tom was permitted to return to Thailand. Since then, March 17 has been celebrated as Muay Thai Day.

The deputy commander Phaya Tak (Taksin) escaped from Burmese captivity and started to re-form the dispersed army units. Within a short period of time he reconquered the old areas and chose Thonburi as the new seat of government. In 1781 Taksin had to be replaced by his officer Phraya Chakri, who ascended to the throne as Rama I in 1782. He relocated the capital and the seat of government from Thonburi to Bangkok. He was the first ruler of the Chakri dynasty, which still governs Thailand today.

Freedom and independence play a very significant role in Thailand's entire history. Even though Muay Thai as a means of defense has decreased in importance due to the development of modern weapons in the 19th and 20th centuries, the position it takes in Thailand's historical development cannot be denied. This is possibly another reason for the passion of many Thais for the sport.

The martial art Muay Thai, developed over centuries, is a very efficient form of self-defense to this day. The techniques used in training can be readily adopted for self-defense. The athletes learn to defend themselves against attacks and to counter, which is why many military and police units are taught Muay Thai.

## Muay Thai Today

Muay Thai is a traditional full-contact type of fighting, which gained ever-increasing importance by fixed regulations after World War II. Thailand features daily fights, which have thousands of spectators.

Athletic competitions have been carried out for centuries. They served as entertainment in honor of the king, and at village festivities for the enjoyment of visitors. Muay Thai continues to be part of festivities today, to which end a ring is put up on a large field. At the end of the event the ring is disassembled and transported to another festival. In this way it is possible to show the fights at small village celebrations.

Champion Thongchai Tor. Silachai hits with a kick.

In the last few years the worldwide interest in Muay Thai went up drastically, reflected by the clearly increased number of athletes attending courses and joining clubs. The development could be due to the staging of high-class martial arts events and the promotion of the cultural heritage of Muay Thai by the Thai government, as well as the increasing popularity of martial art movies and the improved public relations work of the Muay Thai organizations.

## Athletes

Thailand has thousands of professional athletes. They usually come from small villages and grew up in poverty. Their athletic development starts in early childhood, frequently by training and due to encouragement from relatives. The athletes participate in village festivities to earn some money. Successful athletes are accepted into small camps, for which they compete in province stadiums and from where they can be transferred for a small part of the purse to big camps in Bangkok. The biggest part of the purse will be split between the promoter and the fighter. In turn, the fighter passes on a part of his share to his trainer. Despite the share arrangement good fighters can earn much money.

For a professional career the athletes subject themselves to hard training and a very disciplined life. In some camps, for example, the athletes have to sleep on the ring floor and successful fighters enjoy food privileges. Accordingly, only very few foreign athletes in the weight divisions up to welterweight are able to compete successfully with Thai opponents. It is only above welterweight that competitors from countries other than Thailand can be found in the ranking lists of the best Thai boxers. Starting from middleweight, the situation then changes in favor of the foreigners, as Thailand has few athletes of that stature. Against this backdrop fights above welterweight are rarely staged.

The large numbers of Thai supporters are familiar with nearly all the boxers and regularly place bets on their favorites. They follow the fights with great passion, either live or on TV, which features the sport several times a week. Furthermore, nearly all male Thais practice Muay Thai at one stage or another.

The many Thai boxing world championship titles of the different associations can be compared to the titles of the many boxing associations. The government must sanction a valid world championship. Such championship contests are usually conducted in Thailand, which is why high-class contestants also fight in Thailand. Fighters who competed successfully in Thailand are, among others, Ramon Dekker, Danny Bille, Stephane Nikiema, and Rob Kamann. For a Thai boxer admission to and participation in a fight at one of the two principal stadiums, Lumpini and Rajadamnern, is a high honor, which proves the ability of the athlete. If he enjoys great popularity in Thailand, his fight will even be shown on Thai television.

## Events

Thailand has professional fights every day. The leading Muay Thai promoter Songchai Ratanasuban stages the biggest events, which feature the best athletes and attract large audiences wishing to view the interesting fights. Once a year he organizes an open-air event, in honor of the Thai king, which has been attended by more than 100,000 spectators. In accordance with his slogan "Muay Thai—Thai Heritage—World Heritage" he supports the international spread of Muay Thai. At the present time, fights are also staged for women. These fights were established by the Thai promoter and owner of the Muay Thai Institute, Amnuay Kesbumrung.

The Japanese concept of K1 events, in which the best heavyweight full-contact fighters compete, has been successful. The athletic competition fills the biggest Japanese sports arenas. The TV rights are sold internationally, so that the athletes can expect large purses and sponsorship deals. The events are carried out with rules similar to those of Muay Thai. However, hits with the elbows are not allowed, and clinch situations are also stopped at an early stage. Nevertheless, the fights are frequently won by Muay Thai athletes, such as the Dutchmen Ernesto Hoost and Peter Aerts. Due to their small stature Thais do not play a prominent role in Japanese tournaments. The few appearances of Thai athletes in Japan were marked by their extremely hard leg techniques, which even shook opponents who were more than 60 pounds heavier.

Europe and the United States have events with large audiences—for example, in Amsterdam, Paris, Zurich, and Las Vegas. Whether it will be possible to organize regular Thai boxing events with more than 10,000 spectators depends on the level at which such fights can be staged. Muay Thai has the potential to attract all social classes with its thrilling fights over five rounds, in which the athletes use a great variety of spectacular techniques. The concept of a Super League is currently being considered in Europe. Many good fighters in the lower weight categories compete in Europe and excite the spectators with their performance.

Promoter Songchai Ratanasuban.

## Promotion of the Cultural Heritage

The Thai government is intensifying its efforts to promote Muay Thai, the cultural heritage of Thailand. This has become necessary, as the last decades have seen a distinct trend toward a commercialization of the sport. Many managers are interested only in their part of the purse and urge trainers to prepare their fighters for the earliest possible contests. Against this backdrop the athletes no longer undergo comprehensive training but learn only basic techniques. The Thai government now supports the amateur area of Muay Thai with all its facets, in which all the aspects of Muay Thai are taught, thereby not losing the technical diversity of the sport.

The sport is also promoted abroad. This became necessary as more and more types of martial arts started to adapt and/or copy Muay Thai techniques, while keeping the Muay Thai origin a secret. Furthermore, the foreign associations have a more professional approach. They try to present the positive effects of Muay Thai to a broader social spectrum and to do away with the image of Muay Thai as a brutal, unregulated sport, an image that developed due to a lack of knowledge.

The international promotion of the sport has resulted in improved quality of the amateur world championships in Bangkok and in an increasing number of participants. However, the large audiences are missing so far because different associations stage the events and several similar championships are conducted each year.

## Muay Thai as a Fitness Sport

Elements of Thai boxing training are increasingly used in fitness training. Many people have become aware of the manifold effects of martial arts training on physical fitness. Contributing to this awareness are the many successful martial art films, in which the actors amaze the audience with their exceptional skills and perfectly shaped physique. The films frequently show Muay Thai techniques, as these are both realistic and spectacular. This trend was also recognized in Thailand and led to the successful production of the film *Ong Bak,* which was sold to many countries. Tony Jaa, the star in this martial arts film, impresses audiences with his Muay Thai techniques, particularly those deriving from traditional Muay Thai (Muay Boran).

Currently, many celebrities, who like to show themselves practicing Thai boxing, also contribute to the great enthusiasm. Persons conscious of their figures—for example, models and actors who have to stay in their best physical shape for their profession—

are looking for ways to learn this martial art. The demand is satisfied by many sport studios and clubs, which offer many different courses tailored to the individual requirements of their members.

Claudia Hein (Miss Germany 2004) at a training session with the author.

Miss Germany shows a high round kick.

# Chapter 2
# Tradition

Muay Thai has many traditions. The best known are Mong Kon, Pra Jiad, Whai Khru, and Ram Muay. Muay Thai also includes the students' education to become respectful human beings—for example, in their respectful interaction with trainers, the training group, and opponents in the ring.

## Mong Kon

The Mong Kon is a headgear worn by the athlete when entering the ring. It is given to him by his trainer, is meant as a good-luck charm, and should protect him against danger and injuries. Centuries ago the presentation was cause for a celebration, as it was not necessarily commonplace that a person interested in Muay Thai was actually taught. Rather, he was examined by the teacher for a lengthy period of time, and it was only after the teacher was convinced of the character and the physical preconditions of the person that he was given the Mong Kon, thereby being accepted as a student. The Mong Kon was carefully manufactured of white and red fabric, material softer than what is used today.

According to the legend it may never be kept on, held close to, or put on the ground, as it will lose its magic. It is also claimed that the loss of the Mong Kon will have far-reaching consequences for the fighter, because he will lose his self-belief and become sick out of mourning.

In the past the Mong Kon was also worn during the fight. If it fell down, the fight was interrupted until the athlete had put it on again. These days the athletes wear it only at Ram Muay and Whai Khru. After these ceremonies the trainer removes the Mong Kon from the athlete's head.

## Pra Jiad

The Pra Jiad is a piece of cloth worn around the upper arm during the fight. Some athletes wear the Pra Jiad on only one upper arm; other athletes wear one each on both upper arms. Under his Pra Jiad the athlete may carry an object of personal importance, giving him power and self-confidence for the fight. The athlete may, for example, carry a strand of hair from a person very close to him.

Some amateur associations now issue colored Pra Jiads to their members to indicate the performance levels of their athletes (similar to the colored belts in other martial arts, such as Karate). This is a modern development without any traditional Muay Thai background.

(opposite) Trainer Ralf Kussler (www.hanuman-camp.de) presents the Mong Kon to his student Michael Voss.

## Whai Khru and Ram Muay

Whai Khru and Ram Muay are traditional movements performed by the athletes prior to Muay Thai contests. It is often mistakenly assumed that these are Buddhist ceremonies. The Thais take much pride in their traditional performances, which have been handed down for centuries. It is against this backdrop that, out of courtesy, foreign fighters must also perform the Whai Khru and the Ram Muay.

In Whai Khru the athlete kneels on the floor in the center of the ring and expresses his respect to his teacher, relatives, and friends by three bows. During his last bow the athlete concentrates and focuses his thoughts on somebody very precious to him. Immediately after the Whai Khru the athlete starts with the Ram Muay. Ram Muay combines different dance styles in one exercise. In this way the fighters honor their trainer and their gym. They concentrate on, and remember, their own skills and tactics, and their trainer's advice. Ram Muay helps the contestants to calm their nerves and

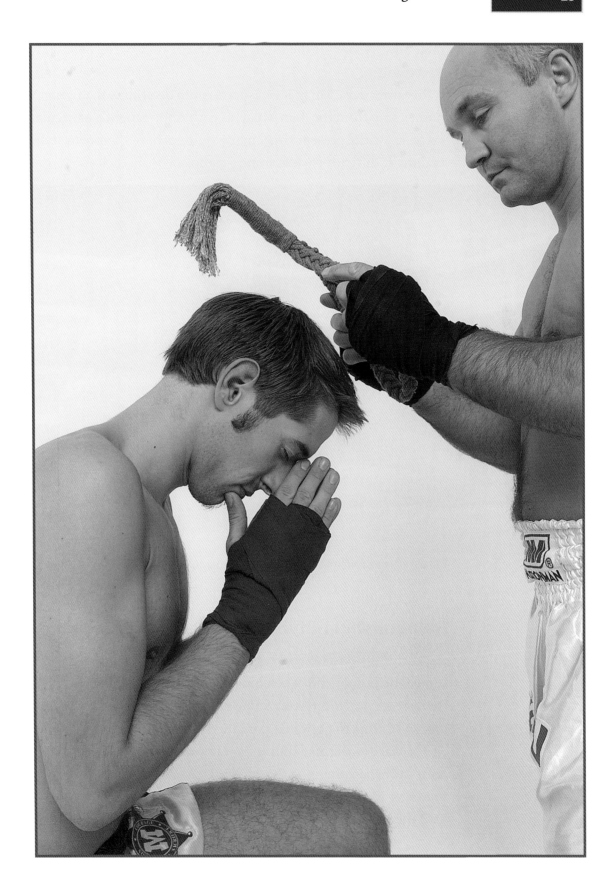

mentally prepare for the fight. The exercise is also a form of body stretching.

In earlier days, Muay Thai experts could determine the fighter's home camp from the Ram Muay, as each camp taught a particular exercise. At the present time, many fighters have their own style, making it difficult to determine a camp.

Female athletes performing the Whai Khru, Rangsit Stadium, 1999.

## Relationship between Student and Teacher

Centuries ago parents interested in Muay Thai introduced their son to the trainer and asked him to accept and train their son. If the teacher was interested, some rules were discussed to enable him to educate the boy in accordance with his ideas.

The teacher accepted him at his camp for some time, and tested him. Only thereafter was the decision made to instruct the boy in the art of Muay Thai. A method to select older applicants was to have them fight each other.

Once the teacher announced that he had made a decision, the boy presented him with some gifts and knelt down in front of him. The teacher expressed his willingness to instruct the new student by putting a Mong Kon on his head. The Mong Kon had to be—and still must be—carefully kept at an elevated position, because it means luck and magic for the student. The Mong Kon was carried in all fights.

After the student had acquired outstanding skills and a great knowledge in Muay Thai, so that his teacher considered him to be able to instruct by himself, a long Buddhist ceremony was conducted. In the process the attendants prayed for luck and protection of the student, who was given a second Mong Kon during the ceremony. Upon presentation of the Mong Kon the student became a teacher.

The Mong Kon was very important for magic and religious reasons. On some occasions, and as a particular honor, the student received the old Mong Kon of his teacher. In that way the new teacher was able to acquire the old teacher's magic and charm. Without the ceremony it was formerly impossible to work as a Muay Thai teacher.

In the course of his life the former student tried to stay in contact with his teacher. Once a year, usually on Muay Thai Day (March 17) or on his teacher's birthday, the student visited his former teacher and presented gifts for his well-being. Many former students are still practicing this today.

## Respect

Muay Thai teaches athletes the respectful treatment of fellow human beings. Respectful dealings with other persons should be the aim of all people. Muay Thai offers a physical advantage in comparison to untrained individuals. The techniques may never be used to suppress others and are to be applied only in self-defense or for the protection of others. The Thais take much pride in their traditional martial art, which helped them to repel intruders in the

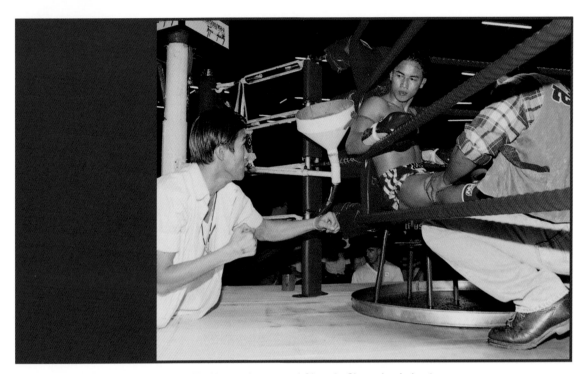

Former Thai boxer, boxer, and Olympic Champion in boxing,
Somlruck Khamsing (left) coaches one of his Thai boxing students.
Many Thai trainers used to be active athletes.

past. They never used the techniques to subjugate other nations. Individuals who learn Muay Thai with the aim of succeeding in their egoistic interests with the help of their physical advantage should be expelled from training. Many centuries ago Muay Thai trainers already considered it to be their responsibility to educate their students in the spirit of being respectful human beings.

## Conduct in Training

The student must be punctual for his training. If, as an exception, he fails to be punctual, he must notify the head of his group and excuse himself.

The athlete's appearance must be neat and he should wear clean clothes for training. Items such as rings, necklaces, and watches must be taken off.

Loud laughter and exclamations should not occur during training. Generally, discussions should only be held with reference to the training.

The trainer's instructions are to be followed. Questions may, indeed, be raised during training but should not be followed up, as this disturbs the training session. The trainer has only a certain amount of time for the session and must also take care of other students. However, in the case of genuine communication problems the trainer will help. It must be understood that an athlete cannot be expected to know all after a few lessons. The learning of Muay Thai is a rather lengthy process, which the masters of the sport claim will never end.

The athletes must treat each other with politeness and respect. They enter training in order to learn the art of Muay Thai. Hurting the partner in training may never be attempted. It is also not the aim to demonstrate any superiority. The actual aim is for the athletes to cooperate, so that a higher performance level can be achieved. If the partner does not adhere to this principle, is more than hard in sparring, and even tries to consciously inflict injuries, you should discuss it with him. If he does not understand, change your training partner. If the trainer insists on a continued "brawl" with this partner, you have chosen the wrong club.

Professional Thai athletes rarely conduct their training at full strength, in order not to sustain any injuries that may prevent them from entering a competition. Otherwise, Thailand would not have active athletes with more than 300 professional fights.

## Conduct during a Fight

The athletes prepare themselves for competition in a long and abstinent process. They welcome each other before the fight, to show respect for their performances as athletes. However, the aim is to win, which is why the athletes may now start to do whatever serves the purpose, provided it conforms to the rules. This may involve intimidation—for example, with aggressive stares. Certain provocations are not acceptable, though. These include insults, spitting, and the conscious use of forbidden techniques—for example, attacks to the genitals. If these are repeatedly carried out by a fighter, he will be disqualified.

After the fight the athletes say goodbye to each other. Both have given their best, and that must be respected.

The athletes conduct their fight at full power.
After the fight they say their goodbyes in recognition
of the performance.

■ Chapter 3

# Rules

Thai boxing contests are subject to strict regulations that vary slightly depending on the venue. Some of the most vital rules are dealt with in this book with reference to the internationally most important stadiums, Lumpini and Rajadamnern Stadiums in Bangkok. More detailed information about these stadiums is found in the book *Muay Thai: Advanced Thai Kickboxing Techniques* (Delp, 2004).

## Important Early Rules

In sports competitions centuries ago the athletes initially used no hand protection. Subsequently, the hands were bandaged. To determine the length of a fight, a small hole was drilled in a coconut shell, and the shell was then put into a container filled with water. The fight was conducted without a break and lasted until such time that the coconut went down. The fight could be decided only by the opponent's technical knockout or knockout; otherwise, the fight would end in a draw. At the beginning of the 20th century the rules were standardized—for example, boxing gloves were used, and a solid ring floor and fixed time periods were prescribed. Furthermore, weight divisions were determined. In the middle of the 20th century the stadiums Rajadamnern and Lumpini were erected in Bangkok. From that time forward, the events could be held at regular intervals and were no longer dependent on weather conditions. At the present time, the stadiums feature daily fights. It is a great honor to compete in these stadiums, which are reserved only for the best athletes.

## Important Current Rules

### Equipment

In the divisions up to and including welterweight the fights are carried out with eight-ounce boxing gloves. Above this weight division ten-ounce boxing gloves are used. The athletes must wear Muay Thai shorts, which correspond to a prescribed design. In addition, they must wear groin protection made of solid material, and a gumshield. Elastic bandages around the joints of the feet are permitted, though not prescribed. Extra elbow, head, and body guards are used in amateur fights. Some associations prescribe shinbone guards.

### Length of the Fight

Professional male fights will stretch over five rounds at three minutes each, with a break of two minutes between rounds. Professional female fights also stretch over five rounds; however, the rounds last only two minutes. The length of amateur fights depends on the promoter and the weight division of the athletes.

### Weight Divisions

The most popular weight divisions in Thailand are the divisions from featherweight up to welterweight, and it is in this range that you will find the majority of active fighters. The classification of the Thai weight divisions corresponds generally to those of the Lumpini and Rajadamnern Stadiums. At an international scale the following classifications are used. Some associations, however, have slightly different weight divisions.

Regular weight monitoring is required. If the athlete must lose too many pounds prior to the fight, he will lack power and energy.

| | | |
|---|---|---|
| Mini Flyweight | above 100 pounds | up to 105 pounds |
| Light Flyweight | above 105 pounds | up to 108 pounds |
| Flyweight | above 108 pounds | up to 112 pounds |
| Super Flyweight | above 112 pounds | up to 115 pounds |
| Bantamweight | above 115 pounds | up to 118 pounds |
| Super Bantamweight | above 118 pounds | up to 122 pounds |
| Featherweight | above 122 pounds | up to 126 pounds |
| Super Featherweight | above 126 pounds | up to 130 pounds |
| Lightweight | above 130 pounds | up to 135 pounds |
| Super Lightweight | above 135 pounds | up to 140 pounds |
| Welterweight | above 140 pounds | up to 147 pounds |
| Super Welterweight | above 147 pounds | up to 154 pounds |
| Middleweight | above 154 pounds | up to 160 pounds |
| Super Middleweight | above 160 pounds | up to 168 pounds |
| Light Heavyweight | above 168 pounds | up to 175 pounds |
| Super Light Heavyweight | above 175 pounds | up to 182 pounds |
| Cruiserweight | above 182 pounds | up to 190 pounds |
| Heavyweight | above 190 pounds | up to 209 pounds |
| Super Heavyweight | above 209 pounds | |

## Legal Techniques and Scoring

The opponent may be hit, kicked, and pushed, to which end all parts of the body can be used, with the exception of the head. The use of elbows is not allowed in fights between women; otherwise, the same rules apply. The amateur area has different performance classifications with varying rules.

Fights are decided either by a knockout, or by three umpires in accordance with a point system.

## Foul

An attack may not be directed toward the genitals, the back, or the eyes of the opponent. Should the opponent fall or the umpire intervene, the technique must be stopped. Holding on to the ropes or deliberately turning one's back in the direction of the opponent,

The umpire jumps in to protect the falling athlete, Lumpini Stadium, 2000.

in order to obtain a break, are not allowed, nor are wrestling or Judo throwing techniques. Unfair conduct, such as biting, spitting, and swearing, will be penalized in the ring. Infringements will be punished with a warning, the loss of points, or disqualification, depending on the type of violation.

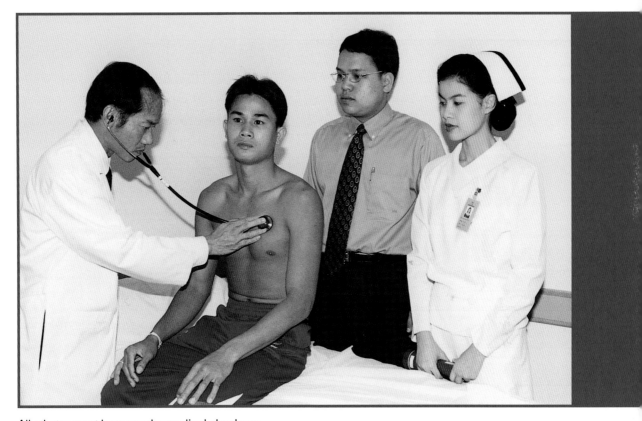

All athetes must have regular medical checkups.

## Medical Support

All athletes must undergo regular medical examinations in order to obtain a license for fights. In addition, shortly before the fight, a doctor examines the athletes for injuries. These checks should also include tests for drugs and infectious diseases, although this is not always done in Thailand.

During the fights, the doctor must be right next to the ring in order to ensure the safety and health of the athletes. If blood is discovered in the eye of a fighter from a cut above the eye or a deep cut elsewhere, the doctor must direct the umpire to stop the fight.

After a knockout, the injured fighter will be suspended for a certain number of weeks. The length of time depends on the type of knockout and possible earlier injuries.

## Music

For many centuries Muay Thai contests have been accompanied by music, which is usually performed by a group of four musicians. On some occasions, however, smaller events with few spectators do not have live music, but play recorded music. Events outside Thailand should also be accompanied by a small group of musicians, so that the traditions of the sport can be maintained.

The music starts as soon as the speaker in the ring has announced the Whai Khru and Ram Muay ceremonies, and lasts until the athletes have ended their performances. Subsequently the speaker issues the order for the fight to start, and the musicians resume playing, though considerably faster. The musicians try to react to the action in the ring, playing slower or quicker, depending on the situation. If the athletic performance is uneventful, they play very fast in order to urge on the fighters. The music is interrupted only during the breaks.

## Whai Khru and Ram Muay

Prior to all fights the athletes perform a Whai Khru and Ram Muay to express their respect for their teachers and their camps. These performances are accompanied by traditional music.

# Chapter 4

# Equipment

The following equipment is used for Muay Thai training. Under normal circumstances each club has a basic assortment of equipment, which is offered to the athletes for training. If you have decided to practice Muay Thai for an extended time period, it is worthwhile to acquire your own equipment. The products suited for your training aims should best be discussed with your trainer. Frequently the trainers have good ties with dealers and are able to obtain products at favorable prices.

## Equipment of the Athletes

### Clothing

Muay Thai training is carried out while wearing a short T-shirt made of cotton or with bare chests. In competition, however, no outerwear may be used. Special shorts, made of nylon or satin, are worn as trousers. These shorts are available in specialized shops, starting from approximately $25. The exercises are carried out with bare feet, as shoes would be a hindrance to the kicking techniques.

### Bandages

In competition and training the hands must be bandaged as prevention against injuries to the hand and finger joints. In competition it is normal to use long bandages, the fitting of which the trainer closely examines. In this way it is ensured that the fighter enjoys the best possible protection and a comfortable fit. For training purposes two short standard tapes from a specialist dealer will suffice. They cost approximately $9.

## Gloves for Sandbags

Sandbag gloves are worn for training on sandbags, punching balls, and pads. These are available at acceptable quality in specialist shops, starting from approximately $40. You can, in fact, also use boxing gloves; however, as these are considerably more expensive, sandbag gloves are normally used for equipment training. One reason to acquire both sandbag and boxing gloves is that in training with a partner and in competition only practically new boxing gloves may be used. The use of damaged gloves entails the danger of injuries to your partner or opponent.

## Boxing Gloves

Training usually requires 16- or 18-ounce gloves as the best possible protection for the athlete and his partner. Small and light boxing gloves are worn in sports contests. Depending on the weight division of the athlete 8- or 10-ounce gloves are prescribed in the rules. In competition the boxing gloves are subject to stricter regulations than in training. This is the reason why the production of gloves for competitive fights is more expensive, which, in turn, is reflected in the price. Boxing gloves for competition are sold starting from approximately $80, and boxing gloves for training from approximately $60.

## Gumshield

In contact training a gumshield is required. For optimum protection it must be adapted exactly to the shape of your teeth. For self-adaptation the least expensive shields are available from approximately $20; however, far more expensive shields are on the market. You can, for example, obtain a gumshield from your dentist after a dental impression for a cost of $300 or more.

## Groin Protection

A blow to your genital area, intentional or unintentional, can result in serious injuries. This is why groin protection must be worn in

The equipment for a professional fight.
The fighter wears a Mong Kon on his head,
which he must take off at the start of the fight.
Around the arms he wears Pra Jiads, and
bandages on his feet.

competition and contact training. The most simple models can be obtained at a price of approximately $20; more expensive models, particularly those for professional boxers, can cost in excess of $90.

## Head Guard

If you exercise techniques to the head during training, a head guard should be worn. Head guards are required for amateur fights; however, they are not used in professional contests. The price for a simple model is approximately $60.

Intensive box sparring warrants the purchase of a very thick head guard, which is on the market for approximately $85. Professional boxers also wear very thick padded models, which are, however, of very high quality and much more expensive.

## Protective Vest

Protective vests with thick padding for sparring are available, so that knee kicks to the body can be practiced. Amateur contests are usually carried out with thin vests; however, they are not used in the professional area. Thick protective vests cost more than $80; thin vests can be obtained from approximately $55. However, the purchase of thin vests is not necessary, as these are usually provided by the promoter.

## Foot and Shinbone Guards

For training you can use foot and shinbone guards. These guards are compulsory for amateur fights. They are not allowed in professional fights. However, bandages around the feet can be used. Simple foot and shinbone guards are available from approximately $30; far more expensive models are on the market. The foot bandages for professional fights are offered from approximately $10.

# Trainer Equipment

A Muay Thai trainer uses different types of pads and belly belts for the training of athletes. These products can be used to teach individual techniques and combinations of techniques. In the case of advanced athletes they also help the trainer to generate situations resembling a fight. He simulates, for example, an opponent's attack by approaching the training athlete with raised pads. The athlete must then step sideways or carry out a number of techniques to the pads to stop the trainer. The trainer also has the opportunity to withdraw, thereby inviting the athlete to follow with the use of techniques. However, newcomers should abstain from these fight simulations; otherwise, the danger of injuries to the pad holder and the training athlete is too great.

The following pieces of equipment are usually available from most of the clubs. They can also be obtained from specialist dealers.

## Boxing Pads

Boxing pads are small pads held in the hands. They are particularly suited for teaching fist and elbow techniques. They are not suited for teaching powerful knee techniques and round kicks, as the pads will not absorb the enormous impact of the hits. Moreover, there is always the danger that the technique may miss the pads or the pads may slip off, thereby hurting the trainer. An artificial leather pad is available from approximately $35, the leather pad from approximately $45.

## Thai Pads

Thai pads are long and thick pads. They were developed for professional training in Thailand to enable the high-power use of all body weapons.

A leather pad with solid filling is offered by the specialized trade from approximately $55. Plastic pads with air fillings are also available, which can be used for the training of women and children. The use of an air-filled pad is not recommended for intensive competitive training, as the kicking athlete will not experience hardening and the trainer must endure the full impact of the hit. An air-filled pad costs approximately $40.

## Belly Belt

During training, a Thai boxing trainer usually wears a belly belt, which is a thick round pad worn around the abdomen and fastened behind the back. The belly belt was developed for the training of athletes in forward kicks and side kicks. Belly belts made of leather and with a solid filling are offered from approximately $80.

Trainer Oliver Glatow shows his equipment. In addition, some trainers also use thick foot and shinbone guards for the intensive training of kicks and blocks.

# Part II

# Basic Skills

Lateral knee kick to the body. The opponent attempts to defend himself with an outstretched arm, Lumpini Stadium, 2000.

# ■ Chapter 1

# Introduction

Beginners in Muay Thai must initially learn the correct *fight position*. From this position the opponent's techniques are warded off, after which the opponent can be attacked with the athlete's own techniques. The fight position is also referred to as "free stance." This means that the athlete rhythmically shifts his weight to the front and rear leg from the position of the initial stance.

Having mastered the fight position, the *steps* will be practiced. Movements to the front, to the back, and to the side are carried out, thereby constantly changing to different *fight distances* and not offering the opponent a fixed target. As long as the athlete is within the fight distance, he must always maintain his fight position.

Only after mastering the initial stance and steps will training of the attacking techniques begin. These are first practiced individually, before the athlete starts to use these in combination. Once the athlete has learned a large number of attacking techniques, he begins to practice a selection of defense and counter techniques. The repertoire of these techniques will be extended step by step, to enable the development of a good athlete.

The fight at close range,
Lumpini Stadium, 2000.

## Basics of Muay Thai
## (Professor Sawang Siripile)

The late Professor Sawang Siripile was the trainer of Ajaarn Somboon Tapina and a large number of important Muay Thai personalities. For a long period of time Sawang Siripile worked as a teacher at the Physical Education College, Bangkok, and, due to his broad spectrum of knowledge, he earned the sobriquet "Father of Muay Thai."

1. Characteristics of a good Muay Thai boxer
   - physically strong, hard, without any physical weakness
   - polite, with athletic spirit
   - clever, strategic
   - powerful attacking

2. Body weapons of Muay Thai
   - fists
   - feet
   - knees
   - elbows

3. Levels of targets
   - low
   - middle
   - high

4. Fighting distance
   - close
   - medium
   - far

5. Timing, fight rhythm
   - quick attack
   - waiting
   - countering
   - pursuing, following

6. Defense of Muay Thai
   - first hit, countering
   - evading
   - blocking
   - holding, clinching
   - maintaining distance

7. Targets of Muay Thai attacks
   forehead, temple, eye, nasal bone, jaw, chin, back of neck, arm (upper part), chest, floating ribs, abdomen, kidney area, backbone, leg (upper part), leg (lower part), solar plexus

Proposed by Assistant Professor Somboon Tapina.

# ◼ Chapter 2

# Starting Position

The student's first training sessions concentrate on the starting position and the Muay Thai steps. The attacking techniques should wait until these have been mastered.

## Stance

In the starting position the stance will be in line with shoulder width. Right-handers move the left foot a little to the front and turn the right foot by about 45 degrees to the outside. This applies in reverse to left-handers. The stance is on the ball of the foot, with the back heel slightly higher than the front heel. The stance on the ball of the foot facilitates quicker moves than a stance resting on the entire foot. You can, for example, take a quick step to the back to avoid an opponent's technique, and you can also take a quick step to the front for countering.

## Guard

Keep the body in an upright position and turn it slightly sideways to the front. At the same time lean the chin slightly toward the chest. The front hand is at eyebrow level and the rear hand slightly above the jaw. The muscles, particularly in the shoulders, are kept loose. At the beginning it is difficult to maintain this hand position over an extended period, as keeping the arms raised is exhausting. After a few weeks of regular exercise the muscles will be strengthened.

You must not lower your guard, even when you are outside the range of attacking techniques. It happens on frequent occasions that a fighter whose guard is down is misled by the opponent and subsequently knocked out by a round kick to the head. Experienced athletes sometimes drop their hands, tempting the opponent to use a technique. However, this is not recommended because of the high risk it entails. Some fighters prefer to hold their hands wide apart and claim that this enables better elbow techniques. This is also not recommended, as the advantage in the execution of elbow techniques is doubtful. Moreover, the athlete must now consciously deflect all the opponent's straight punches, which is difficult, particularly when he tires in a fight.

## Look

Aim your eyes at the central part of your opponent's body. Do not concentrate on one point, but try to focus on the entire body. It is

Ajaarn Somboon Tapina demonstrates the correct starting position.

thus more possible to foresee which body weapon the opponent will use for his next attack. In close distance (punch, elbow, and clinch techniques) aim your eyes at the head of your opponent, so that possible moves can be detected at an early stage. In a clinch situation you do not need to look down, as you can notice the beginning of a knee kick by the opponent's rotation of his body, provided you are close to the opponent in accordance with the correct clinch technique (see pages 119–130).

## Muay Thai Starting Position/Fight Position

1. The stance is on the ball of the foot, not on the entire foot.

2. Right-handers have a leading left hand, left-handers a leading right hand.

3. Always keep your guard up; the hands must never drop.

4. Relax your guard somewhat and don't tense your muscles, so that quick moves are possible. The muscles should be kept tense only once the opponent's attack has been detected.

5. Always protect your chin.

6. Observe all parts of the opponent's body. Do not concentrate on one point.

7. Maintain the optimum fight distance, neither too close nor too far away.

8. Take steps to the front, to the rear, and to the side.

## Typical Mistakes

■ The front hand is held far outside or the hands are too low. The fighter is unable to defend himself against swift attacks to the head—for example, by straight punches.

■ The hands are dropped when tired. As the fighter is then unable to fully concentrate, he is particularly prone to knockout techniques. When tired, particular attention must be maintained to holding the hands high.

■ The weight is resting on the soles, instead of the balls, of the feet. It is difficult to change distances quickly if the athlete is not on the balls of his feet.

■ The eyes are fixed on only one point of the opponent's body. The fighter must, instead, observe the entire body of his opponent, at continuously changing points, to be able to detect the start of a technique.

Fight position, Rangsit Stadium, 2000.

# ■ Chapter 3

# Steps

Now that you have learned the fight position, you can start learning the Muay Thai steps. The steps are used to approach the opponent, to move away, or to evade an attack. During the entire process you remain in the fight position. The front foot must be aiming toward the target, and the rear foot must be at an angle to the outside. This also applies to a lateral approach toward the opponent. Do not tense up during your moves, and pay attention to your guard. For greater agility many athletes carry out the steps on the ball of the foot.

You should initially practice the forward and backward moves, after which you integrate the lateral moves in your training. Repeat the steps several times under the supervision of your trainer. Then you can perform your footwork freely. When doing so, imagine a fight with a real opponent. If he attacks, you move to the side or to the rear. For your own attacks you move several steps to the front.

The footwork must be practiced as a separate unit, at least in the first hours of training. The perfection of the footwork is a precondition for the use of attacking, defense, and counter techniques. If, for example, you intend to bridge the distance to the opponent for the use of a technique, you must take a quick step forward.

For learning the footwork and shadow boxing it is best to define an area—for example, the size of a boxing ring—and to practice within the boundaries. If you reach one of the borderlines, you move away with lateral steps.

# Forward and Backward Movement

## Forward

The front foot moves forward; the rear foot follows along the ground.

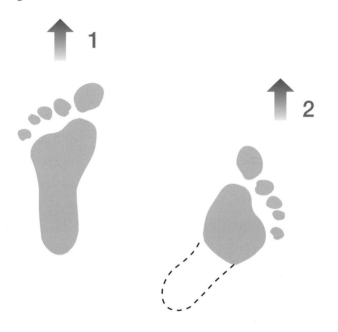

## Backward

Move your rear foot to the back and follow with the front foot.

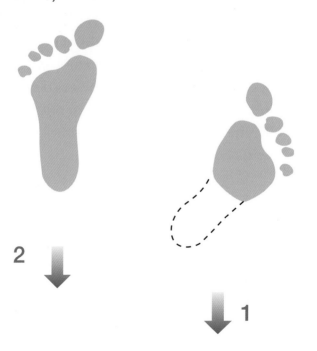

## Semi-Circle Movements

For the application of this technique the opponent will be approached sideways. This is recommended when the opponent, for example, approaches while punching or kicking. This way you get out of reach of the opponent's body weapons and you are able to counter. At the end of this move you will be facing the opponent at an angle of between 45 and 90 degrees, your feet will be the same distance apart as in the starting position, and the toes of the front foot will be directed toward the opponent.

### Step to the Left

You initially position your left foot to the front left, then follow with the right foot. For a left-hander it requires a change to an orthodox stance, before the left-hander stance can be resumed in a next step.

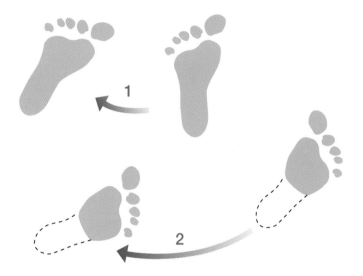

### Step to the Right

You initially position your right foot to the front right, then follow with the left foot. For an orthodox boxer it requires the change to a left-hander stance, before the orthodox stance can be resumed in a next step.

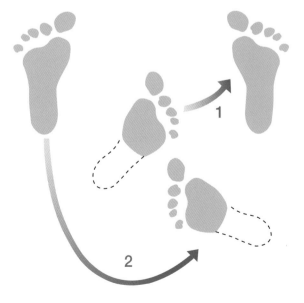

# ▪ Chapter 4

# Fighting Distance

A fighting distance is considered to be a distance within reach of your opponent. No direct techniques can be delivered at a distance of more than 5 feet between individuals of average height. The attacker must first take a step in the direction of his opponent, or he must jump toward him, before he can use a technique. The opponent, however, can avoid the fight by taking one step to the back or moving to the side.

If the fighters are not within the safety distance, they are in the so-called fighting distance. The fighting distance is divided into three groups: long, half, and close range.

Full contact with a round kick from long range, Rangsit Stadium, 2000.

## Long Range

The use of kicks is predominant—for example, forward kicks, side kicks, and jump kicks. To use a hitting technique, you must initially take a step forward. A suitable way to bridge a long distance, or to move away from the opponent, is to combine the step with a jab. By means of a hard kicking technique you can move the opponent out of the immediate fighting distance.

## Half Range

Punch techniques, knee kicks from a distance, and kicks are carried out. Aggressive athletes are looking for the distance to attack the opponent with many different combinations. The opponent can try to move back and out of this distance, or he can narrow the distance with a step to the front in order to clinch. Thai athletes frequently watch each other at half range and try to determine the strengths, weaknesses, and reactions of their opponents.

## Close Range

The distance is mainly used for hooks from the side, uppercuts, and elbow techniques. These techniques are carried out continuously, until such time that one of the two athletes succeeds in moving away or getting a hold of the opponent's neck for clinching. In clinch situations knee kicks and throws are used.

## For the Boxer
## (Phrases from Renowned Trainers)

- "Prerequisite for a good fighter is exhaustive technical training." (Ajaarn Somboon Tapina)

  The athlete should initially undergo comprehensive technical training before he enters competition. Many athletes try to compensate for their lack in basic techniques by power and instinct. A high-ranking position, however, can never be achieved without good techniques.

- "To be a good fighter you have to master the basic techniques, must be in excellent physical shape and self-assured, and must not be nervous when entering the ring." (Ajaarn Somboon Tapina)

  Deficits in any one of these areas render successful participation in tournaments unlikely. Therefore, the athlete must prepare himself in the best possible way, so that he can enter the ring assured of his own skills.

- "Before you defeat the opponent, you defeat yourself." (Ajaarn Somboon Tapina)

  For successful fights the athlete must already "torture" himself in training. This includes intensive training, weight control, and an appropriate lifestyle.

- "To win or to lose a fight is not of overriding importance, if you prepared yourself for the fight in the best possible way." (Ajaarn Somboon Tapina)

  Hard training is a precondition for participation in a competitive fight. If the athlete has given his best in preparation and competition, he can be proud, even if he loses the fight.

- "In a contest both fighters spray water, both become wet, however, one more than the other. You must be better than your opponent to become less wet." (Professor Sawang Siripile)

  Both athletes deliver and receive blows in a fight. Each athlete must be aware that he will also be hit.

- "Good fighters never show their pain." (Professor Sawang Siripile) "No part of the body must be weak or injured." (Ajaarn Somboon Tapina)

  Competitors may never show their pain; otherwise, the hurting part of the body will be attacked without mercy. Furthermore, the opponent must not be able to identify a weak point, as he will exploit the situation.

- "You should not become angry in a fight; otherwise, the heart will pound, but the eyes remain blind." (Ajaarn Somboon Tapina)

  An athlete fighting without control and concentration will always be in danger of a counterattack.

- "If you realize in a fight that the opponent is stronger, you will win through the spectators." (Ajaarn Somboon Tapina)

  For the score sheet the athlete must merely convey the impression of being the stronger fighter. This is the reason why some athletes smile after they have been hit.

# Part III

# Attacking Techniques

A hard blow with the shinbone to the head frequently leads to a knockout,
Bangkok, 1999.

# ◼ Chapter 1

# Introduction

Novices are first instructed in the basic stance. On the basis of this stance they learn how to approach an opponent and how to move away. It is then necessary to practice the basic attacking techniques.

Prior to and after the execution of attacking techniques, you will also be in the fight position. All steps in the course of the attacking techniques are carried out as described in Part II. For example, in order to cut the distance, a straight punch is frequently combined with a step in the direction of the opponent.

You should first practice the attacking techniques slowly and deliberately, without an opponent and without interruption. (The following illustrations show the techniques in several steps, for better understanding. However, this does not mean that the respective technique should be interrupted.) At the beginning, the kicking techniques are practiced at stomach or chest level. Once the agility of your body has improved after several weeks of regular training, you can also practice the techniques to the head.

The umpire restarts the fight after a break. The female athletes take a fight position, Rangsit Stadium, 2000.

If you succeed in the correct execution of the techniques into the air, you can also include sandbag training in your program. In the process, the techniques are initially practiced separately, before they are combined with each other. After gaining experience practicing on the sandbag, and once you have learned, for example, to stabilize your wrist on impact, you can also practice the techniques on pads and with a partner.

## Points of the Body Particularly Prone to Injuries

### FRONT VIEW:

| | |
|---|---|
| 1. temples | 2. forehead |
| 3. eyes | 4. nasal bone |
| 5. lateral center of the jaw | 6. point of the chin |
| 7. larynx | 8. collarbone |
| 9. point of the sternum | 10. solar plexus |
| 11. lower rib | 12. unprotected abdominal tissue |
| 13. genital area | 14. upper adductor area |
| 15. knee joint and kneecap | |

All target areas can be used for self-defense. However, some restrictions apply in competition—for example, the opponent may not be hit in the genital area. The exact regulations vary from promoter to promoter.

Training should be conducted with a partner. It is not the aim to injure the partner and to show him your superiority. Therefore, techniques to knockout points should never be carried out at full strength.

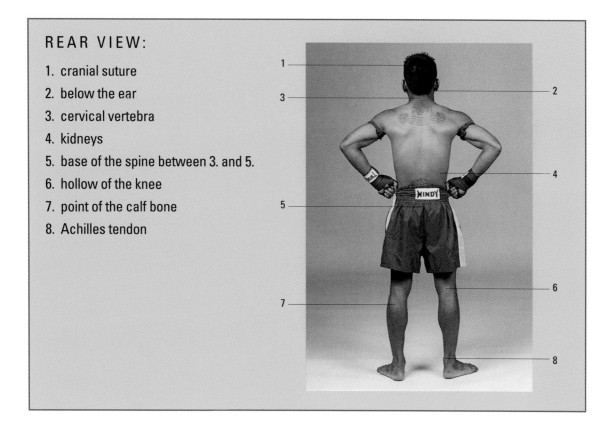

**REAR VIEW:**

1. cranial suture
2. below the ear
3. cervical vertebra
4. kidneys
5. base of the spine between 3. and 5.
6. hollow of the knee
7. point of the calf bone
8. Achilles tendon

## Usable parts of the body

Fists, elbows, shinbones, feet, and knees may be used in Muay Thai.

**A:** The fist techniques are carried out with the knuckles. To avoid injury, always pay attention to a firmly closed hand.

**B:** The tip of the bone is used for elbow techniques, as this is the hardest point. Blows delivered with the tip of the bone may cause bleeding—for example, on the forehead—which may frequently result in an early termination of the fight.

**C**: The leg techniques are carried out with the shinbone. Fast techniques can also be delivered with the instep. For example, to provoke the opponent with a quick kick to the head.

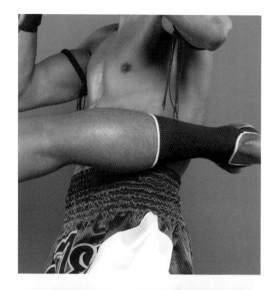

**D**: Straight foot techniques are carried out with the ball of the foot. For hard contact you can also use the heel or the entire foot. Lateral techniques are carried out with the entire foot.

**E**: Knee techniques are carried out with the kneecap, if possible, at the maximum length of the knee.

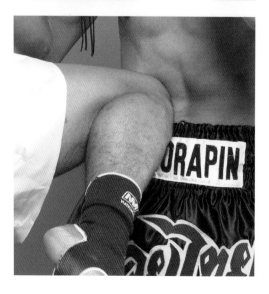

# Chapter 2

# Fist Techniques
# (Chock)

When delivering punches in Muay Thai the legs remain stretched, in contrast to other types of martial arts, so that the attack can be continued promptly. As a matter of principle you should try not to lower your height; otherwise, you are susceptible to knee techniques to the head.

Stand on the ball of the foot, and aim your eyes at the target. During execution both the shoulder and the hip are turned. If the punch makes contact, enforce the blow by shifting the weight to the front leg. Deliver your punches with the knuckles in a horizontal position. In the process protect your chin with the raised shoulder, and the face with the non-hitting hand. Punching power

The fighter defends himself against a straight punch by leaning the upper part of his body to the left. It is strongly recommended not to use this technique, as it provides the opponent with the opportunity of a knee kick to the head.

derives from speed of execution, weight shifting, and the turn of the hips and the shoulder. Subsequently, you promptly return to the starting position.

Ensure that you do not retract the hand prior to a punch, as the opponent will anticipate your technique at an early stage. The punch must also be explosive and should not be "pushed."

Keep your hand open, fingers stretched. First close the fingers and ensure they are tight. Thereafter, press the fingertips somewhat into the palm of your hand. Finally, put the thumb across the index and the middle fingers. The blow is delivered with the knuckles of the upper half of the fist. The knuckles of the index and middle fingers must absorb the main load.

## Fist Techniques

| | | |
|---|---|---|
| 2.1 | Straight Front Punch/Jab | Mat Jab/Mat Throng Chock Num |
| 2.2 | Straight Rear Punch | Mat Throng/Mat Throng Chock Tam |
| 2.3 | Uppercut | Mat Ngad/Mat Seri |
| 2.4 | Side Hook | Mat Hook/Mat Weang Sun |
| 2.5 | Hook to the Body | |
| 2.6 | Overhead Punch | Mat Kook |
| 2.7 | Swing | Mat Weang Yao |
| 2.8 | Spinning Backfist | Mat Weang Glab |

## ■ 2.1 Straight Front Punch/Jab
### (Mat Jab)

> **Targets: Nose, Chin, Eyes**

### Execution:

The technique is started from the fight stance by slightly raising the heel of the rear foot.

You now deliver the front fist in a direct line toward the opponent. The elbow should be held down as long as possible; otherwise, the opponent will notice your technique at an early stage and will be able to defend himself. The rear fist remains in the starting position above the jaw for protection against the opponent's techniques. In the process of the punch, turn the hip and shift your weight to the front for powerful execution of the technique. Shortly before contact, turn the fist so that the palm is facing the floor. After the punch, quickly return the fist to the starting position.

**A–C:** *The straight punch with the front arm, also referred to as the jab.*

Use the punch as often as possible, to disturb the opponent's timing.

A

B

C

A

B

C

# ■ 2.2 Straight Rear Punch
## (Mat Throng)

> Targets: Nose, Chin, Eyes,
> Solar Plexus, Stomach

## Execution:

You are in the fight position. Start the technique by slightly raising the heel of the rear foot.

You now deliver the rear fist in a straight line toward the opponent. The elbow should be held down as long as possible; otherwise, the opponent will notice your technique at an early stage and will be able to defend himself. The front fist is kept above the jaw for protection against the opponent's techniques. In the process of the punch, turn the hip and shift your weight to the front for powerful execution of the technique. Shortly before contact, turn the fist so that the palm is facing the floor. Ensure that the punch is explosive and not pushed. After the punch, quickly return the fist to the starting position.

**A–C:** *Somchok demonstrates the straight rear punch.*

# ■ 2.3 Uppercut
## (Mat Ngad/Mat Seri)

> **Targets: Chin, Ribs, Solar Plexus**

## Execution:

You are in the fight position. Drop one of the lower arms and turn the fist so that the lower and the upper arm form a rough right angle. In the process you shift your weight to the active side and bend your knees somewhat. The other fist is kept above the jaw for protection against the opponent's techniques.

Now you abruptly hit from below, while stretching the legs, turning the body and the hips, and shifting your weight to the front. Ensure that you hit the target with the knuckles and that the punch is not interrupted on the way up. Subsequently you quickly return the fist to the starting position.

**A–C**: *The uppercut with the rear arm.*

In contrast to boxing, the knees should not be bent much for an uppercut in Muay Thai, as it would facilitate an opponent's knee kick to the head.

A

B

C

A

B

C

## ■ 2.4 Side Hook
### (Mat Hook/Mat Weang Sun)

> **Targets: Jaw, Temples, Ribs, Ears**

### Execution:

Starting from the fight stance you raise one fist sideways, so that the arm is nearly parallel to the ground. At the same time you shift the weight to the leg of the active side of the body and slightly lean sideways with the upper part of the body. Keep your other fist above the jaw in order to block possible techniques of the opponent.

You now carry out a lateral punch move, in the process of which you turn the body and the hips in the direction of the punch and shift your weight in the same direction. Subsequently, you quickly return the fist to the starting position.

**A–C**: *The side hook with the rear arm.*

The technique is carried out at a close distance to the opponent. The swing, in contrast, is delivered from a long distance.

## ■ 2.5 Hook to the Body

> **Targets: Ribs, Solar Plexus, Stomach**

### Execution:

Starting from the fight stance you drop one of the lower arms and turn the fist, so that the lower and the upper arm are nearly at a right angle to each other. At the same time, shift your weight to the leg on the active side and lean slightly with the upper part of the body to this side. Keep the other fist above your jaw as protection against the opponent's techniques.

Deliver your fist abruptly to the target, in the process of which you turn your hip and shift the weight of your body to the front. Subsequently you quickly return the hitting hand to the starting position.

**A–C:** *Somchok demonstrates a body hook to the stomach with the rear arm. He could also aim for the ribs. In that case it can also be delivered as a side hook.*

A

B

C

**A**

**B**

**C**

# ■ 2.6 Overhead Punch
## (Mat Kook)

Targets: Nose, Forehead, Eyebrows

## Execution:

Starting from the fight stance you raise the rear fist. You then deliver the fist in a wide arch from above to the target. Keep the front fist above your jaw as protection against the opponent's techniques. During the punch, turn your hip to the inside and shift your weight to the front, for powerful execution of the technique. In the process you turn the fist in such a way that the palm of the hand faces the floor on impact. Subsequently, you quickly return the fist to the starting position.

**A–C:** *The punch above the head. This technique is carried out using the rear fist.*

## ■ 2.7 Swing
### (Mat Weang Yao)

> **Targets: Jaw, Temples, Ribs, Ears**

### Execution:

Starting from the fight stance you raise one fist to the side. At the same time, shift your weight to the leg on the active side of the body and lean your body slightly to this side. Keep your other fist above the jaw for protection against possible techniques of your opponent.

You now deliver a wide lateral punch, simultaneously turning the body and the hip in the direction of the punch and also shifting the weight of your body in the same direction. Subsequently, you quickly return the fist to the starting position.

**A–C:** *Chawan demonstrates the swing.*

The technique is similar to the side hook. In contrast to the side hook, it is delivered from a long distance and carried out with a wide swinging movement. The swing is, in fact, a powerful technique; however, it is relatively easy to anticipate. For this reason swings are hardly ever seen in the ring.

A

B

C

A

B

C

# ◼ 2.8 Spinning Backfist
## (Mat Weang Glab)

> **Targets: Jaw, Temples, Ears**

### Execution:

You are in the fight position. Move your front leg forward to the inside and shift your weight to it.

You then quickly turn across your front foot, at which time you try to get the opponent back in your line of vision as soon as possible. Starting from the orthodox stance you perform a clockwise turn. In the case of a left-hander stance you have to rotate counter-clockwise. Use the power generated by the rotation to deliver the rear arm toward the opponent. Contact is made with the knuckles of the fist. Subsequently you quickly return to the fight stance.

**A–C:** *The rotating backhand fist punch with the rear arm.*

The technique is usually delivered with the rear arm. However, if the opponent moves away, the technique can also be delivered with the front arm. It is fairly difficult to use the technique with success, which is why it is rarely seen in competition.

## Frequent Mistakes

- The punch is delivered with an open fist. This entails the danger of damage to the capsules. The athlete must close the fingers with the thumb firmly placed on top.
- The athlete does not watch the effect of the punch and misses the use of other techniques.
- The athlete does not remain in one line during the punch, but steps to the side. The punch cannot be carried out with full power.
- The punch is "pushed" and not delivered in an explosive motion. The athlete is unable to retract his guard quickly enough, and the opponent has the opportunity for an effective counter.
- The jab is carried out without the use of the body weight and a shift of the body toward the opponent. The punch cannot be delivered with full power.
- On delivery of the punch with the front or rear arm, the elbow is raised. Frequently the arm is also initially pulled back before the punch is delivered. The opponent foresees the punch and can defend himself.
- The punch with the rear arm is restricted to the arm movement, without a turn of the hips. The punch will lack power.
- The uppercut is delivered from far behind. The opponent is now able to hit you first with one of his techniques.
- The athlete loses his balance on delivery of a side hook. For powerful execution, the athlete may, indeed, jump somewhat toward the opponent, but he should not lose his balance. If the opponent has not been hit with a powerful blow, he may deliver an effective counter.
- The rear foot slips away when delivering combinations of techniques. The athlete loses his balance to some extent and falls forward due to the weight shift.
- In the course of a punch the athlete drops the hand raised for protection. The opponent may now deliver an effective counter. If he recognizes that this happens repeatedly, he will await his chance for a premature end of the fight.

# Chapter 3

# Elbow Techniques (Sok)

The elbow is a very hard body weapon with short reach. Its use can result in a knockout or a bleeding head. If the opponent already has a wound on his forehead, you can rub your elbow knuckle in the wound in the course of further elbow techniques, thus achieving a premature end to the fight. The special characteristic of the elbow techniques is that, even when they fail, it will be difficult for the opponent to deliver effective kicks or punches in return. This is due to the close stance. However, much training is required before it is possible to use elbow techniques with success.

Each elbow technique can be used twice, on the way to the target and on the way back. However, a successful elbow technique frequently requires a quick step forward. The step should be quick; otherwise, there will be less power in the technique and the opponent will be able to defend himself. When using the rear elbow, an additional step forward with the rear foot is possible. The elbow techniques must be completed and may not be stopped at impact or after a miss. The blow is delivered by the knuckle of the elbow, as it is very hard. Ensure that your chin is protected by the raised shoulder, and that the body and legs are stretched. The free hand protects against the opponent's attacks. Power in the delivery of the technique is generated by the possible step to the front, the speed of execution, use of the shoulders, and the shifting of weight behind the technique.

Although the photos show the techniques only to one side, they can be carried out with the left and the right elbow.

## Elbow Techniques

| | |
|---|---|
| 3.1 Rotating Elbow/Hitting Down Elbow | Sok Tee |
| 3.2 Side Elbow | Sok Tad |
| 3.3 Uppercut Elbow | Sok Ngad |
| 3.4 Spear Elbow | Sok Pung |
| 3.5 Reverse Elbow | Sok Kratung |
| 3.6 Spinning Elbow | Sok Glab |
| 3.7 Elbow from Above | Sok Sub |
| 3.8 Elbow after Jump from the Thigh | Sok Yeap |

The elbow technique misses the opponent's head.

# 3.1 Rotating Elbow/Hitting Down Elbow

## (Sok Tee)

| Targets: Forehead, Nasal Bone, Eyebrows |
| --- |

## Execution:

From the fight position you raise one elbow sideways, until the tip of the elbow is aiming upward. The fist of the other arm is kept above the jaw for protection against the opponent's techniques. The body weight is evenly distributed to both legs.

You now hit your elbow from above to the target, with a concurrent and analogue turn of the upper body and hips. The weight is transferred to the front. Deliver the technique in such a way that the motion is fully completed, even if you miss the target. To this end, the hand of the active arm is pulled through below the shoulder of the other arm. Subsequently, you quickly return to the fight position.

**A–C:** *Patiphan demonstrates the rotating elbow.*

The technique is often used in fights, as it can be delivered behind the opponent's guarding hands.

A

B

C

**A**

**B**

**C**

## ■ 3.2 Side Elbow
### (Sok Tad)

> **Targets: Jaw, Temples, Nasal Bone**

### Execution:

You are in the fight position. Raise one arm shoulder high. The fist of the other arm is kept above the jaw for protection against the opponent's techniques. The body weight is evenly distributed to both legs.

You now deliver your arm horizontally to the other side, while turning the foot of the active side, the hips, and the upper body in the same direction and shifting the weight to the front. Impact is made with the knuckle of the elbow. The technique should be carried out in such a way that the delivery is completed, even if you miss your target. To this end the fist of the hitting arm passes the raised and guarding arm on the outside. Subsequently, you return to the fight position.

**A–C:** *The side elbow.*

The technique is frequently used in clinch situations if the opponent has slightly dropped his guard.

# ■ 3.3 Uppercut Elbow
## (Sok Ngad)

| Targets: Chin, Nose |
| --- |

## Execution:

From the fight position you slightly lower one of the elbows. In the process, shift your weight to the leg on the active side and bend it somewhat. The fist of the other arm is kept above the jaw as protection against the opponent's attacks. The body weight is evenly distributed to both legs.

You now deliver your hit with the elbow knuckle to the target, retracting your hand past the ear toward the shoulder. In the course of the technique, you stretch the leg and the upper body and turn the hip to the inside. At the same time shift your weight to the front. Ensure that you complete the blow to the top, and do not stop or interrupt the technique. Subsequently, you quickly return to your fight position.

**A–C:** *The uppercut elbow is carried out in a straight line from below.*

As an alternative, you can also deliver the hit at a 45-degree angle, which will render you less susceptible to counter attacks. It will, however, result in less power. The technique is particularly suited to using the rebound of the rope for momentum.

A

B

C

A

B

C

## ■ 3.4 Spear Elbow
### (Sok Pung)

Targets: Nasal Bone, Forehead,
Eyes, Collarbone

### Execution:

From the fight position you raise one hand past the ear. The other hand is kept above the jaw for protection against the opponent's techniques. The body weight is evenly distributed to both legs.

You now deliver the blow to the target from above at a 45-degree angle. In the process you stretch the upper body and shift your weight toward the opponent. The impact follows with the knuckle of the elbow. Subsequently, you quickly return to the fight position.

**A–C:** *Patiphan demonstrates the spear elbow with the rear arm.*

## ■ 3.5 Reverse Elbow
### (Sok Kratung)

> **Targets: Jaw, Chin, Solar Plexus, Stomach**

**Execution:**

From the starting position you turn your front lower arm down, so that the elbow is aiming toward the opponent. The other hand is kept above the jaw for protection against the opponent's techniques. The body weight is evenly distributed to both legs.

You now deliver the blow with the elbow knuckle from below. In the process, you stretch your body in the direction of the opponent, which will raise your rear foot. At the same time shift your weight to the front. Subsequently, you quickly return to the fight position.

**A–C:** *Chawan demonstrates the reverse elbow with the front arm. The delivery originates from the attack position.*

The reverse elbow is mostly used after a rotating or side elbow has missed the target. This will then lead to an immediate counter blow.

A

B

C

A

B

C

## ■ 3.6 Spinning Elbow
**(Sok Glab)**

> Targets: Chin, Jaw, Temples,
> Eyebrows, Ears

### Execution:

You are in the fight position. Move your front leg to the inside front and shift your weight to it.

You now perform a rapid turn across your front foot, trying to regain sight of your opponent as quickly as possible. From the orthodox position you turn clockwise. If, however, you start from the stance of a left-hander, you must rotate counter-clockwise. Use the energy generated by the rotation to hit your opponent with the rear arm. The blow is delivered with the elbow knuckle. Subsequently, you quickly return to the fight position.

**A–C:** *The rotating elbow with the rear arm. Patiphan performs a clockwise rotation.*

The technique is usually delivered with the rear elbow but can also be applied by the front elbow.

If you miss the opponent, turn your body around its own axis, thereby automatically returning to the starting position.

# ■ 3.7 Elbow from Above
## (Sok Sub)

> **Targets: Head, Nasal Bone, Collarbone**

## Execution:

From the starting position you shift your weight to the front leg. In the process, stretch your body upward and raise the rear arm far to the top. At the same time, turn the rear part of your body to the front.

You now deliver the elbow down to the target, using the weight of your body. Impact is made by the elbow knuckle. Subsequently, you quickly return to the fight position.

**A–C**: *Somchok demonstrates the elbow from above.*

The technique is usually carried out with the rear arm, although the front arm can also be used.

The elbow from above is similar to the spear elbow. The difference is that the elbow is raised far to the top and the heels are raised higher, thus enabling a blow from a higher position for greater impact. In addition, this is not a 45-degree blow, but contact is made from above.

The technique is also frequently delivered in combination with a jump.

**D**: *The elbow from above can also be delivered to the head or the collarbone using both elbows.*

A

B

C

D

**A**

**B**

**C**

## ■ 3.8 Elbow after Jump from the Thigh (Show Technique)
### (Sok Yeap)

> **Targets: Head, Nasal Bone, Collarbone**

### Execution:

From the fight position you step with the front foot onto the opponent's upper leg. In the process, grab the opponent's neck with your front hand, to stabilize your position. Jump with the front foot and raise the rear arm far to the top.

You now deliver the elbow to the target, using the weight of your body. Impact is made with the elbow knuckle. Ensure that you safely return to the floor, where you quickly resume your fight position.

**A–C:** *The elbow after take-off from the upper leg.*

The technique was applied centuries ago, as, in some types of Muay Thai, the fighters used to take a very low stance. At the present time, however, it is accepted that for greater efficiency in a contest, the athletes should stay upright as far as possible. Against this backdrop, the technique is no longer applied in fights, but is popular in Muay Thai shows.

## Frequent Mistakes

- The athlete stops the elbow in motion, not completing it. He is unable to deliver the technique at full strength. As a matter of principle, all techniques must be completed in the direction of the movement. A side elbow, for example, is completed to the other side if it misses the opponent. In an unfavorable position, the athlete can protect himself with a reverse elbow.

- The fist is tightly closed during the elbow techniques, which applies tension to the muscles of the arm. The athlete is unable to deliver the technique swiftly. In all elbow techniques the muscles should remain relaxed and should be tensed only at the moment of impact.

- The athlete does not use any weight for the elbow technique and does not shift his body in the direction of the opponent. This way he is unable to deliver a powerful technique.

- The athlete does not use the knuckle of the elbow, but the softer part slightly above on the upper arm. The opponent is not hit with any great power, and the athlete may even injure himself.

- The rear foot slips away in the course of combinations. The athlete loses his balance and falls forward due to the weight shift to the front.

- The guarding hand is dropped in the process of a technique. This entails the great danger of a knockout, if the opponent steps to the side and counters with, for example, a side hook.
  Particularly in elbow techniques a high guard is very important, as, due to the short distance, it is difficult to react properly to the opponent's attack. The only means of defense is frequently the block with raised hands.

- The athlete does not guard his chin with the raised shoulder of the elbow arm. If the opponent leans back, he has an effective point for a counter in front of him.

# Chapter 4

# Kicking Techniques / Kick (Te)

The round kick in Muay Thai differs from the kicks in other martial arts. It is delivered wide from the outside, and contact is made with the shin. Attention must be paid to an inside turn of the hip, and the weight must be included in the technique. The kick may be delivered to any part of the body, from the feet to the head.

It is recommended that the hands are kept high for defense against the opponent's techniques, so that punch techniques can be delivered after the kick. As an alternative, you can stretch the front arm to keep the opponent away.

However, many Muay Thai trainers instruct their students to pull their arm down during the kick, thus giving added power to the use of the hip and strengthening the kick. This, however, requires

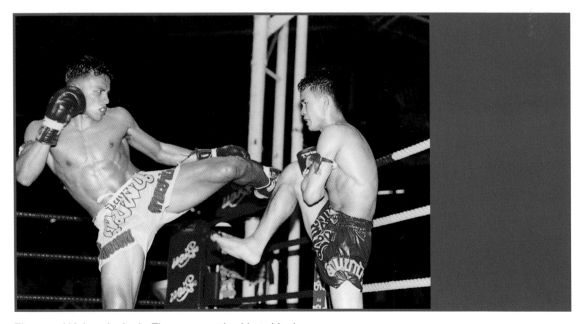

The round kick to the body. The opponent is able to block this attacking technique.

a very high shoulder, and the other hand must be held in front of the face; otherwise, the opponent has an easy target.

Although the photos show the technique from only one side, they can be carried out with the left and the right leg.

## Kicking Techniques

| | | |
|---|---|---|
| 4.1 | Leg Kick | Te Ka, Te Tad Lang |
| 4.2 | Round Kick to the Body | Te Lam Toa, Te Tad Glang |
| 4.3 | High Round Kick | Te Sung, Te Karn Koa |
| 4.4 | Half-Shin, Half-Knee Kick | Te Khrung Khang Khrung Khow |
| 4.5 | Heel Kick from Above | Te Kook |
| 4.6 | Spinning Heel Kick | Te Glab Lang, Chorake Fard Hang |
| 4.7 | Jumping Round Kick | Grad Dod Te |

A

B

# ■ 4.1 Leg Kick

## (Te Ka, Te Tad Lang)

> **Targets: Upper Leg, Knee, Lower Leg**

### Execution:

You are in the fight position. Move one leg somewhat to the outside front and shift your weight to it.

You then apply the kick in a semi-circle to the target. In the process, turn the pivot leg farther to the outside and add the hip and the body weight to your kick. Impact is made with the lower end of the shinbone. Pay attention to your guard, as a powerful delivery will leave you vulnerable to the opponent's counter punches. Subsequently, quickly return your leg to the fight position.

**A–C:** *The kick to the outside of the upper leg.*

**D:** *The kick to the inside of the leg. The kick is also carried out with the shinbone. For assessment of the fight distance, you can also kick with the instep.*

C

D

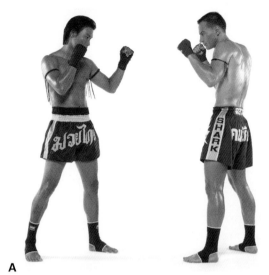

**A**

**B**

**C**

## ■ 4.2 Round Kick to the Body
### (Te Lam Toa, Te Tad Glang)

> **Targets: Ribs**

### Execution:

From the fight position you approach the target in a semi-circle. In the process, the pivot leg is resting on the ball of the foot and turns along to the outside. The technique makes contact once the highest point of the semi-circle has been passed—in other words, slightly from the top down. Deliver the kick in such a way as if you were kicking through an object, and use your hip and the weight of your body to the full extent. At the moment of impact the kicking leg will be stretched, to obtain the optimum in kicking hardness. Contact is made with the shinbone. Subsequently, quickly return your leg to the fight position.

**A–C:** *Somchok demonstrates the round kick to the body with the rear leg. In the process, he delivers the front arm somewhat from the top. During delivery the face must be protected by the raised shoulder and the rear hand. However, it is recommended that you keep your hand in front of the face for protection, or stretch it out toward the opponent, to keep him away.*

## ■ 4.3 High Round Kick
### (Te Sung, Te Karn Koa)

Targets: Temples, Jaw

### Execution:

From the fight position you approach the target in a semi-circle. In the process, the pivot leg is resting on the ball of the foot and turns along to the outside. The technique makes contact once the highest part of the semi-circle has been passed—in other words, slightly from the top down. Deliver the kick in such a way as if you were kicking through an object, and use the hip and the weight of your body to the full extent. At the moment of impact, the kicking leg will be stretched, to obtain the optimum kicking strength. Contact is made with the shinbone. Subsequently, quickly return your leg to the fight position.

**A–C**: *The high round kick with the shinbone.*

The technique is sometimes carried out with the instep, for a faster kick. The aim is to provoke the opponent with a kick to the head, so that he starts an uncontrolled attack.

A

B

C

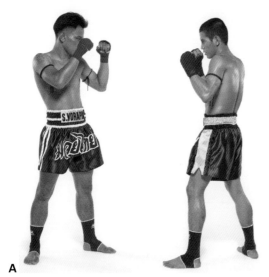

A

B

C

## ■ 4.4 Half-Shin, Half-Knee Kick
### (Te Khrung Khang Khrung Khow)

> **Targets: Stomach, Chest, Ribs**

### Execution:

You are in the fight position. Slightly retract one leg and deliver it in a bent position toward the target. In the process, the pivot leg is resting on the ball of the foot and turns along to the outside. When hitting the target, move your hip to the front and slightly lean back with your upper body. Contact is made with the upper part of the shinbone and the knee. Subsequently, quickly return your leg to the fight position.

**A–C:** *Chawan demonstrates the half-shin, half-knee kick.*

The technique is applied when the opponent approaches, as it can be delivered from a short distance. A straight knee kick could also be used. To avoid a clinch, which frequently follows a knee kick, the opponent can be pushed away by the pictured technique.

# ■ 4.5 Heel Kick from Above
## (Te Kook)

> **Targets: Center of the Head, Collarbone**

### Execution:

From the fight position you shift your weight to the front leg. Quickly raise your rear leg in a wide arch from the inside, until it is far above the target. Keep your leg muscles relaxed. At the same time, the heel of the pivot leg is raised and the pivot leg turned to the outside.

You now deliver the leg with the use of the hip in a powerful move from above, while tensioning the leg muscles. Contact is made with the heel. Ensure that you don't drop your guard when dropping the leg. Subsequently, quickly return to the fight position.

**A–C:** *The heel kick from above with the rear leg.*

The kick can also be carried out with the front leg; however, delivery with the rear leg is more powerful.

A

B

C

# ■ 4.6 Spinning Heel Kick
## (Te Glab Lang, Chorake Fard Hang)

> **Targets: Temples, Jaw, Ears, Neck**

### Execution:

You are in the fight position. Move your front leg to the inside front and shift your weight to it.

You now rotate across the front foot, while trying to regain sight of your opponent as soon as possible. From the orthodox stance you make a clockwise rotation; from the opposite stance you move counter-clockwise. In the process, raise your leg and turn the pivot leg so that the heel is pointing toward the target. In the final phase of the rotation, deliver a circular kick from the outside to the opponent's head. Stretch your leg, and carry out the kick with the

A                                B

lower leg, supported by the hip. Contact is made with the heel. Subsequently, the kicking leg returns as the front leg to the floor and is pulled back before resuming the fight position.

**A–D**: *Patiphan demonstrates the rotating heel kick with the rear leg and with a clockwise rotation.*

The technique is usually carried out with the rear leg but can also be performed with the front leg.

C

D

A

B

C

## ■ 4.7 Jumping Round Kick
### (Grad Dod Te)

> **Targets: Temples, Jaw, Neck, Upper Arms, Ribs**

### Execution:

Starting from the fight position, slightly bend your knees, shift your weight to the front leg, and commence the jump. In the process of the jump you deliver the rear leg with the support of the hip to the target. At the moment of impact, the leg is stretched for optimum hardness of the kick. Point of contact is the shinbone. Pay attention to a controlled return to the floor, first with the jumping leg. Subsequently, return to the fight position.

**A–C:** *The jumping round kick with the rear leg.*

The technique can also be carried out with the front leg, but with less power.

## Frequent Mistakes

- The athlete does not deliver the round kick in a semi-circle, but initially bends the knee; thereafter, he carries out a snapping movement with the foot. This variant of the kick is, indeed, common in some martial arts. However, that way it is not possible to kick with optimum hardness.

- When missing the opponent, the turn of the semi-circle kick is completed, whereby the athlete will end up with his back to the opponent, offering an easy target. After a miss the athlete should change the stance of the pivot leg from the ball of the foot to the entire foot, thereby stopping the rotation.

- Contact is made with the instep, and not with the shinbone. The athlete is unable to deliver a powerful kick, and he is even in high danger of injury—for example, if the opponent blocks a round kick to the body with the shinbone. Kicks to the leg or head can sometimes be carried out with the instep, if the intention is to deliver quick instead of strong kicks aimed at provoking and destabilizing the opponent.

- The athlete drops his hands while kicking. The guard must always be kept high; otherwise, the opponent may counter with effective hits. Furthermore, with hands held low it is difficult to follow up with a quick punch right after the leg has returned to the floor.

- The hips are not turned to the inside in a kick. For a powerful delivery of a kick the hip must always be turned to the inside as much as possible and the weight must be included in the kick.

- The athlete is leaning backward during a kick. He is unable to put his weight into the kick and cannot follow up with a straight punch.

- The athlete does not stretch his pivot leg at the moment of impact. He is unable to perform the kick with the greatest possible strength.

- The stance is not on the entire foot, or the pivot leg is not stretched. It is difficult for the athlete to turn the pivot leg, and he is unable to fully use his hips.

# Chapter 5

# Pushing Foot Techniques (Teep)

Good foot techniques can make fights a lot easier, as they can be used for attack and defense. With these techniques you can disturb the opponent's timing and balance, and may even succeed in a knockout. Generally speaking, foot techniques should be used frequently to occupy the opponent and to disturb his timing for attacking techniques. To this end, more attention must be paid to a quick delivery than to kicking power. However, each one of the following kicks may be used for a premature end of the fight, if it is delivered with the appropriate power.

The fighter succeeds in a surprise attack and delivers a kick to the head.

The techniques initially target the knee, before you deliver this leg with hip support to the opponent. As an alternative you can also kick the stretched leg directly from the floor to the target, but this does not provide the same power. For kicks it is important to use the hip and the body weight for extra power. At the same time, you move on the ball of the foot, which enables you to increase the speed and power of kicks. Always pay attention to raised arms for protection. It is often possible to accidentally slide into the opponent due to a mistaken assessment of the distance or the turn of the pivot leg.

The kicks can be carried out with the front or rear leg. The front leg can be used at the start of the fight in order to disturb the opponent's timing, the rear leg for kicking the opponent on approach. You have to decide by instinct which of the following kicks you use in each situation. To this end, regular practice of the kicking techniques is essential.

## Pushing Foot Techniques

| | | |
|---|---|---|
| 5.1 | Straight Front Kick | Teep Trong |
| 5.2 | Front Kick to the Leg/Jab Kick | Teep Robgaun |
| 5.3 | Side Kick | Teep Khang |
| 5.4 | Back Kick | Teep Glab Lang |
| 5.5 | Jumping Front Kick | Grad Dod Teep |

# ■ 5.1 Straight Front Kick
## (Teep Trong)

> **Targets: Stomach, Solar Plexus, Chest**

### Execution to the Body:

You are in the fight position. First pull one knee toward your chest and aim the foot in the direction of the target. If you carry out the technique with the rear leg, you also turn the rear part of the upper body to the front. Keep your guard up for protection against the opponent's techniques.

You now kick with the support of your hip toward the opponent. In the process, turn your pivot leg to the outside and slightly lean back with the upper part of your body. Contact is made with the ball of the foot, the heel, or the entire foot. Subsequently, you quickly pull back the knee to the upper part of the body before you return the leg to the floor.

**A–C:** *The front kick to the body with the rear leg. The heel or the entire foot is used for hard impact.*

The front leg is normally used for the technique with the ball of the foot, as this enables rapid kicks, which can stop the opponent's attack. However, all of these variants may be carried out with the front or rear leg.

A

B

C

D

E

F

## ▪ 5.1 Straight Front Kick *(continued)*
## (Teep Trong)

> **Targets: Chin, Face, Larynx**

### Execution to the Head:

You are in the fight position. Pull one knee toward your chest and aim your foot toward the target. If the technique is carried out with the rear leg, also turn the rear side of your body to the front. The guard remains up for protection against the opponent's techniques.

You now deliver a kick with the support of your hip. In the process, turn your pivot leg to the outside and slightly lean the upper part of your body back. Contact is made with the ball of the foot, the heel, or the entire foot. Subsequently, pull back your knee toward the chest before you return the leg to the floor.

**D–F:** *The front kick to the head.*

If you succeed in hitting the opponent with a foot technique to the head, it will provoke him, frequently leading to an uncontrolled attack, which can effectively be countered. The kicks are normally delivered with the ball of the foot.

For hard blows and a possible premature end of the fight it is best to kick with the heel to the chin. However, this variation requires long and intensive training.

# ■ 5.2 Front Kick to the Leg/Jab Kick

## (Teep Robgaun)

> **Targets: Knee, Thigh, Lower Leg**

## Execution:

You are in the fight position. Slightly pull back the front knee and aim with the ball of the foot at the target. Keep your guard up for protection against the opponent's techniques.

You now kick the opponent with the support of your hip. In the process, somewhat turn your pivot leg to the outside. Contact is made with the ball of the foot, the entire foot, or the heel. You then quickly pull back your knee before you return the leg to the fight position.

**A–C:** *The front kick to the leg.*

The kick can be used frequently to disturb the opponent's timing. Continuous kicking will interrupt the opponent's preparation and delivery of techniques. Only 50 percent of the available power is used. Should the opportunity arise to kick through the opponent's leg, 100 percent must be put into the kick. To this end, the technique can also be carried out with the rear leg.

The technique is also possible with the foot held sideways, which facilitates contact.

A

B

C

A

B

C

## ■ 5.3 Side Kick

### (Teep Khang)

> **Targets: Stomach, Solar Plexus, Chin, Nasal Bone**

### Execution:

Starting from the fight position you pull one knee toward the chest and slightly turn the pivot leg to the outside. If you carry out the technique with the rear leg, simultaneously turn the rear side of your body to the front.

You now kick your opponent with the support of your hip and a lateral turn of the pivot leg. At the same time, turn the pivot leg farther to the rear and lean back the upper part of your body. Contact is made with the heel or the entire foot. Ensure that the guard is not neglected. Subsequently, quickly retract the knee toward the chest and return the leg to the floor.

**A–C:** *Somchok demonstrates the side kick.*

In Muay Thai, in contrast to other martial arts, the body is not completely turned to the back.

# ■ 5.4 Back Kick
## (Teep Glab Lang)

> **Targets: Stomach, Solar Plexus, Chin, Nasal Bone**

## Execution:

You are in the fight position. Move one leg to the inside and shift your body weight to it.

You now turn your back in the opponent's direction, concurrently turning the pivot leg to the rear. At the same time, bend the other knee. Starting from the orthodox position you turn clockwise, from a left-hander stance counter-clockwise. You then kick the opponent with the raised leg supported by the hip. Some athletes initially look at the opponent after the rotation; others kick instinctively. Contact is made with the heel or the entire foot. Subsequently, the knee is bent back before the leg returns to the floor.

**A–D**: *Patiphan demonstrates the rear kick. He turns clockwise.*

The technique can also be used after a round kick has missed the target. From this position you must promptly step back, without prior retraction of the knee. The variation is applied by instinct for protection in a critical situation. This is why the kick cannot be delivered with power.

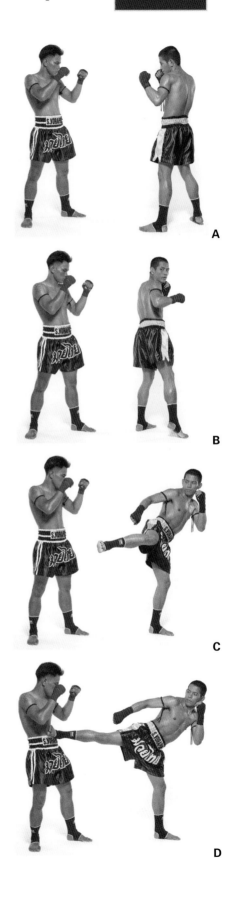

A

B

C

D

**A**

**B**

**C**

# ■ 5.5 Jumping Front Kick
## (Grad Dod Teep)

> **Targets: Chest, Chin, Face**

### Execution:

You are in the fight position. Shift your weight to the front leg, bend it, and use it for the jump off the floor.

In the process of the jump, pull your rear leg toward your chest and turn the rear part of your body to the front. You now deliver a straight kick to the target, supported by the use of the hip. Contact is made with the ball of the foot, the heel, or the entire foot. Subsequently, you make a controlled return to the floor and return to the fight position.

**A–C:** *The jumping front kick, carried out with the rear leg.*

The front leg can also be used for the technique, but with less power.

## Frequent Mistakes

- The athlete briefly keeps the leg up in the air after impact, instead of a prompt retraction and return to the floor. The delivery enables the opponent to hold on to the leg and to apply a throw technique.

- In the course of a kick, the athlete drops his guard. The guard must always be kept high, or the opponent will then be able to deliver effective counter techniques. The opponent could, for example, deflect the kick to the side and succeed in a knockout with a high round kick to the head. In addition, a low guard will render it difficult to promptly follow up with a straight punch after the return to the floor.

- The front kick is carried out with a pronounced backward position of the upper body. When using the hip the athlete may, indeed, slightly lean back with the upper body, but not too far, as he will then be unable to deliver the kick with utmost strength.

- The kick is delivered without the support of the hip. For a powerful execution the athlete must always use the hip and also put his weight into the kick.

- On delivery of the kick the athlete stands on a bent pivot leg and the entire foot. However, the pivot leg should be stretched and somewhat on the ball of the foot. This facilitates a turn for optimum use of the hip. Furthermore, if the athlete misjudged the distance, he will be able to make quick minor adjustments to his stance.

- When kicking with the ball of the foot, the toes are not pulled back and the ball is not pushed out. If the toes make contact, they can easily be overstretched and the capsules could be hurt.

- The athlete takes an uncontrolled forward fall after the kick. The kick must, in fact, be hard and the body weight must be used; however, the athlete must always be in control of his technique.

# Chapter 6

# Knee Techniques from a Distance (Khow)

The knee is one of the most dangerous weapons in Muay Thai. Experts in knee techniques can achieve a knockout with a single blow. The legendary Thai top fighter Dieselnoi, for example, mastered the knee techniques to a degree that enabled him to succeed in many early knockouts and, in the end, it was nearly impossible to find an athlete willing to fight him. To be able to reach perfection in the techniques, the same as for the Thai athletes, you not only have to carry them out correctly, but you also have to practice them time and again for timing and power. The knee can be used for attack, but also as protection with a block.

The knee is a body weapon with short reach. Prior to the use of a knee technique you should, therefore, know the distance to your

The fighter succeeds with a jumped knee kick to the head. Only a few fighters are able to deliver the technique with success.

opponent. You can then hold one hand in front of the opponent's face, in order to find out whether the distance is suitable for a knee kick, and also for irritation of the opponent. If possible, hold the opponent's neck and pull him toward you, which will render the knee kick more effective. For better defense it is usually the left hand that holds the opponent's left part of the neck, or the right hand at the right part of the neck. It must be borne in mind, though, that the hold should never be attained with a concurrent grip of both hands, as this will make you vulnerable to, for example, an uppercut. The hold must always initially be achieved with one hand, and only use the second hand when it comes to a clinch.

The power of the techniques derives from the take-off, speed, and use of the hip. For a more powerful kick, it is also possible to jump. It is important to stretch the body, to be able to rest on the ball of the foot.

The knee kick is one of the most important body weapons for self-defense, with the preferred target of the genital area in many of the following knee techniques.

### Pushing Foot Techniques

| | |
|---|---|
| 6.1  Straight Knee Kick | Khow Trong |
| 6.2  Diagonal Knee Kick | Khow Chiang |
| 6.3  Flying Knee Kick | Khow Loy |
| 6.4  Knee Kick after Jump from the Thigh | Khow Yeap |

# ■ 6.1 Straight Knee Kick
## (Khow Trong)

> **Targets: Stomach, Solar Plexus, Chin**

### Execution with the Rear Leg:

You are in the fight position. Deliver your knee in a direct line toward the opponent, while raising the heel of your pivot leg and turning the pivot leg to the outside.

On contact, shift your hip forward and lean back the upper part of your body. Due to the stance on the ball of the foot, the stretched pivot leg, and the support from the hip, the knee will cover the longest possible distance to the opponent. Ensure that you do not drop your hands. Subsequently, quickly return to the fight position.

**A–C:** *The straight knee kick with the rear leg.*

For irritation of the opponent, you may hold your front hand briefly in front of his face.

A

B

C

D

E

F

## ■ 6.1 Straight Knee Kick *(continued)*
## (Khow Trong)

> **Targets: Stomach, Solar Plexus, Chin**

### Execution with the Front Leg:

You are in the fight position. Initially move your front leg to the back, from where you promptly deliver it toward the opponent. A powerful delivery of the technique can also be carried out with the front leg.

In the course of the kick you lift the heel of the pivot leg and turn the pivot leg to the outside. On impact, shift your hip to the front and lean back the upper part of your body. Due to the stance on the ball of the foot, the stretched pivot leg, and the support of the hip, the knee travels the longest possible distance to the opponent.

**D–F:** *Somchok demonstrates the straight knee kick with the front leg. Starting from the fight position he moves the front leg to the rear and follows up with a prompt knee kick. In the photo Christoph approaches him with one step.*

*If Christoph were to move away, Somchok could follow, change his stance by moving the rear leg to the front, and, thereafter, he could deliver a kick with the other leg.*

# ■ 6.2 Diagonal Knee Kick
## (Khow Chiang)

Targets: Ribs, Stomach, Head

### Execution:

From the starting position you try to gain a diagonal hold of the opponent's neck. To this end, the left hand holds on to the opponent's left side, or the right hand to the right side. If you succeed, slightly pull the opponent in your direction.

You now deliver a lateral kick from the same side of the body up to the target, while lifting the pivot leg and turning the pivot leg to the outside. On impact you move your hip forward.

**A–C:** *Patiphan demonstrates the lateral knee kick. He approaches Chawan with one step and slightly pulls him forward by the neck. If Chawan were to approach him rapidly, he could also deliver the lateral kick without pulling.*

A

B

C

A

B

C

## ■ 6.3 Flying Knee Kick
### (Khow Loy)

> **Targets: Solar Plexus, Chin, Face**

### Execution:

You are in the fight position. Shift your weight to the front leg, bend it, and use this leg for take-off.

In the course of the jump you deliver your rear leg in a straight line to the target. At the moment of contact, shift your hip forward for powerful delivery of the technique. Ensure that you do not drop your guarding hands. Subsequently, you return in a controlled move with the take-off leg first to the floor, and resume the fight position.

**A–C:** *Patiphan demonstrates the jumping knee kick.*

The technique is particularly effective if the opponent rebounds from the rope after a previous hit.

## ■ 6.4 Knee Kick after Jump from the Thigh (Show Technique)

### (Khow Yeap)

> **Targets: Chin, Face**

### Execution:

Starting from the fight position, step with your front foot onto the opponent's thigh. Hold his neck to stabilize your position, and jump with your front foot.

You now deliver your knee to the target with the support of your hip, while pulling the opponent's head in your direction. Ensure that you return to the floor in a controlled move. Subsequently, quickly return to the fight position.

**A–C:** *The knee kick after take-off from the thigh.*

This knee kick was used centuries ago, as in some types of Muay Thai the athletes used to take on a deep squat position. At the present time, however, it is accepted that athletes should adopt a rather stretched stance in contests. Against this backdrop, the technique can no longer be observed in fights but is popular in Muay Thai shows.

A

B

C

## Frequent Mistakes

- The knee kick is carried out with a pronounced backward position of the upper body. On use of the hip the athlete may, indeed, slightly lean back with the upper body, but not too far, as he will then be unable to add his weight to the kick.

- The athlete does not add his weight to the knee kick. However, for a powerful delivery of the knee kick he must include the hip and his body weight in the technique.

- On delivery of a knee kick the knee is moved forward far from the pivot leg. This leaves the athlete open to the opponent's defense and counter techniques. It is for this reason that the knee must be moved forward close to the pivot leg.

- On delivery of the knee kick the athlete is resting his weight on the entire foot of the pivot leg, instead of raising the heel. He is unable to turn the body to the front, and the knee kick cannot be delivered at maximum reach. In addition, the acceleration generated by the take-off from the heel cannot be used.

- The athlete does not stretch the knee or the pivot leg. Instead, he must straighten up as far as possible, to be able to make use of the knee technique's complete reach. By delivery of a pointed knee he can deliver an effective blow, and the danger of injury due to an opponent's technique decreases, as the muscles are tense.

- The athlete neglects his guard by lowering his arms in the process of a technique. Due to the close distance in knee kicks, the athlete must always protect himself against fist and elbow techniques and may never drop his guard.

- On use of the hip and leaning back of the upper body, the head is overstretched to the rear. Instead, the larynx must always be protected, which is why the chin must be lowered somewhat toward the chest.

# Chapter 7

# Clinch Techniques
# (Garn Goad Plum Tee Khow)

Knee kicks can be delivered from a distance or in clinch situations. The term "clinch" describes fight situations in which the athletes are at a close distance to each other and use a hold for knee kicks. The better your hold, the more effective your attacks with knee techniques will be.

In a first clinch situation during the fight, both athletes will deliver knee techniques. If one of the contestants turns out to be clearly weaker in clinching, he will then try to avoid any further clinches. If the opponent, however, succeeds in getting a hold of him, the weaker fighter frequently just concentrates on moving the hip to the inside, thereby lessening the effect of the opponent's kicks. At the beginning of a new kick he can throw the opponent

The fighter attempts to control her opponent with a hold around the neck, and delivers a knee kick.

in the direction of the kick, or in the opposite direction. Subsequently, he can continue with the fight from a different distance (see page 170).

In a self-defense situation, different from the following explanations, the fingers will be interlocked for added pressure. In addition, the knee technique to the genitals can be carried out.

The successful application of clinch techniques requires intensive and lengthy training.

---

### Clinch Techniques

Basic Stance

Optional Clinching Grips

Knee Techniques

Control

---

## ▧ 7.1 Basic Stance

With the basic technique you try to be as close as possible to the opponent. Raise your shoulders and lower your chin slightly toward the chest for best possible protection of the larynx against the opponent's elbow techniques.

Your stance is on the ball of the foot, the feet are approximately shoulder width apart, and your body weight is evenly distributed to both feet. The position is best suited to compensate for the opponent's changes in pressure and to avoid throws.

Stretch your body upward and slightly to the rear. This stance facilitates knee techniques. Techniques at a close distance have a lesser effect, or may not even be possible at all. Furthermore, the high position enables you to apply maximum pressure to the opponent's head.

One hand will be placed on the back of the head, the wrists touching, and the other hand will be placed diagonally for added pressure. As an alternative, you can also hold on to your own elbow. It is important that the arms are in front of the opponent's chest, in order to be able to control him by brief left and right movements. In this way you protect yourself against the opponent's body weapons. A rapid move can also throw the opponent to the side. This is best done if the opponent applies a knee technique from the outside.

The clinch favors the fighter who is able to place his grip between the opponent's arms. Thus, it is easier to control the opponent. This is why the athlete with his hands on the outside repeatedly attempts to move his hands to the inside, thereby pushing away the arms of his opponent. For this move, only one hand should be used, while the other continues to apply pressure to the opponent's head. The hand pushes the opponent's arm from above or below and tries to find its direct way to the opponent's head from the inside. Once the corresponding position has been reached, an attempt is made to follow with the other hand to the inside.

If the opponent succeeds in placing both hands from the inside around your neck, and he thus has the better clinch position, stretch your body in his direction. In the process you try to hold on to him. Should this not be possible around the neck, take a hold around his shoulders or hip.

*The ideal position for the clinch. Chawan (left) has his holding grip from the inside around the neck and can thus control Patiphan by moving his neck to the left and right.*

## Gripping

To bring about a clinch situation, you initially apply a hold with only one hand. Try to get a hold of the opponent's neck. If you succeed, you protect your position by shifting your hip in the opponent's direction, and only then you apply a hold with the second arm. The simultaneous use of both arms will leave you open for uppercut or elbow techniques, as your head is unguarded.

**A–C**: *Patiphan demonstrates the way to a clinch. He initially applies a hold around Chawan's neck with the front hand. It would be better to gain a hold from the inside if the opponent has an open guard or is in the early stage of a punching technique. He now pulls Chawan's head and protects his position by moving toward him and holding on with the second arm. He is now able to pull Chawan's head down and can deliver an effective knee kick.*

A

B

C

## ■ 7.2 Optional Clinching Grips

On principle, in a clinch the athletes will try to apply the inner grip. If unsuccessful, you can use one of two optional techniques by which the opponent can also be effectively held.

### Grip to the Ribs

Basically, this technique can always be used in a clinch but is particularly suited against tall opponents. Take a hold of your opponent with both hands rib high and cross your hands on his back. As an alternative you can grip your own elbow, thereby stabilizing the position. Press hard against the opponent's ribs, so it becomes difficult for him to breathe. You now slightly retract one leg and deliver the knee to the stomach, ribs, or thigh. In addition, you can apply pressure with the chin to the shoulder blade, or, in the case of a very tall opponent, you can push your head toward his chin to inflict pain.

**A–B:** *Patiphan demonstrates the grip to the ribs.*

A                   B

## Diagonal Grip

In this technique you take a diagonal hold of the opponent. To this end, you have to place one arm above the shoulder, the other arm below the shoulder, after which you cross your hands behind the back of his head. In addition, you can apply pressure with your chin to the opponent's shoulder blade. Push the opponent somewhat to the side, whereby one of the sides will be unguarded, and deliver a knee kick to this side.

**C–D**: *Patiphan demonstrates the diagonal grip.*

C

D

A

B

C

## ■ 7.3 Knee Techniques

From the basic clinch stance you can attack the opponent with a straight knee kick to the stomach, or with a lateral knee kick to the ribs. You can also deliver a blow to the thigh from the front or the side.

If you succeed in pulling the opponent down, one leg will be retracted and then delivered from below with the support of the hip.

### Straight Knee Kick

From the basic stance you slightly retract one of the legs to the rear, pulling the opponent along. You now deliver it with hip support in a straight line to the opponent's stomach.

**A–C:** *Chawan has taken a hold with the inner grip. He retracts his leg, pulling Patiphan along. He then delivers a knee kick.*

## Lateral Knee Kick

Starting from the basic stance you initially retract one leg somewhat to the side, after which you deliver it to the opponent's lower rib. Deliver the kick in a diagonal line from below.

As an alternative, you can also kick in a round arch to the ribs. This enables very hard kicks; however, it is also easier for the opponent to block the technique.

Another option is a kick with the inside of the knee. In the process the knee will be delivered to the opponent's body from far outside.

**A–B:** *Chawan carries out a lateral knee kick. It could also be delivered in a round arch or with the inside of the knee.*

## Low Knee Kick

Starting from the basic stance you slightly retract one leg, after which you deliver it to the front or, from the outside, to the opponent's thigh.

The technique is used to disturb the opponent's timing. It can, for example, block the beginning of an opponent's knee kick. This does not require a powerful execution. The technique can also be used to deliver an effective blow.

**C–D:** *Patiphan delivers a knee kick to the central part of the thigh.*

A

B

C

D

A

B

C

## ■ 7.4 Control

If you succeed in a clinch to get a hold of the opponent's neck from the inside, you can control the opponent by pulling and pushing prior to an effective hit.

### Throw to the Outside

Following on from the inner grip position in a clinch, push the opponent's neck to the left and right, which leaves him in an uncontrolled position. You now deliver knee kicks, which he is hardly able to fend off.

**A–C:** *Patiphan has applied the inner grip to Chawan's neck. He now controls Chawan by pushing him to the left and right. Subsequently, Patiphan is able to deliver effective knee kicks.*

## Pulling along to the Rear

You are in the starting position for a clinch and have placed your lower arms around the opponent's neck from the inside. You now move one leg to the rear, while pulling the opponent along and his head down. Deliver a knee kick with the retracted leg to the opponent's chin. This frequently leads to a knockout. If you do not succeed in pulling the head down, deliver a kick to the body.

**A–B:** *Patiphan has applied the inner grip and slightly retracts one leg, while pulling Chawan's head. Subsequently, Patiphan delivers a knee kick to the head.*

## Pulling along to the Side

You are in the starting position for a clinch and have placed your lower arms around the opponent's neck from the inside. You now move one of your legs to the outside front. You follow with the other leg and pull the opponent along with you. It is now possible to deliver an effective knee kick.

**C–D:** *Patiphan moves his leg outside right. He now retracts his former front leg and pulls Chawan along. Subsequently, he delivers a knee kick to the body.*

A

B

C

D

## Frequent Mistakes

- In a clinch the athlete reaches out to the opponent's neck with both arms. The athlete will now be susceptible to uppercuts or elbow techniques, as his head is unguarded. He must, instead, initially reach out with one hand, and the second hand follows only after he succeeds in getting a hold and slightly pulling the opponent toward him.

- The athlete does not place the hand on top of the other wrist for fixation of his hold on the opponent's neck. He misses out on the leverage for pulling the opponent's head down.

- The body is not stretched inside up toward the opponent and the stance is not on the ball of the foot. The athlete is unable to apply maximum pressure to the opponent. It will now be easier for the opponent to push the athlete's head down, and to deliver a knee kick to the head for a premature end of the fight.

- During clinching the athlete has his feet wide apart. He will be unable to stretch his body to the inside, thus enabling the opponent to push him down with the head—for example, in combination with a step to the outside.

- The athlete has his legs too close to each other in a clinch. He will be unable to compensate for changes in the direction of the pressure, and the opponent can throw him to the side.

- The body weight has been shifted to one leg and is not evenly distributed to both legs. Once the opponent realizes this, he will throw the athlete to the side.

- The athlete has applied an inner grip; however, the opponent succeeds with a grip in between. To defend his position against this attempt, the athlete can slightly raise the elbow on the side attacked by the opponent.

- The athlete does not protect his chin below the raised shoulder. At a close distance elbow techniques will always be possible. For this reason, the athlete must minimize the attackable area insofar as is possible, and he must guard his chin.

- The athlete stretches his head upward, thereby offering the larynx as a target for an attack. For protection of the larynx, the athlete must always pull his chin somewhat toward the chest.

# Part IV

# Combination of the Attacking Techniques

Knockout by a left hook from the side. The look is glazed and the guard is completely down. Lumpini Stadium, 2000.

# Chapter 1

# Use in Training

The training of combinations enables a quick sequence of attacking techniques. These are practiced during shadow boxing, on the sandbag, on pads, and jointly with a partner. The combinations must be practiced time and again. In a fight situation—be it in competition or self-defense—you will not have the time to consider consciously which techniques to use and how to combine these with each other. You will use only the techniques and combinations that you have frequently practiced, and that you are now able to perform instinctively. The trainer may, for example, provide advice during breaks, pointing out the athlete's and the opponent's mistakes. It is, however, the fight itself that dictates the use of techniques.

In professional boxing, once the opponent has been named and his weaknesses and strengths have been analyzed, certain combinations and fight plans will be practiced. If the opponent, for example, has a powerful straight punch, a Thai boxing trainer will repeatedly teach the combination of attacking techniques with foot and knee kicks to the side of the opponent's punching arm.

The following chapters deal with some of the combinations that are frequently trained in Muay Thai. The abbreviation *l* stands for the left side and *r* for the right side. It is assumed that the reader is using an orthodox stance—that is, he is a right-hander. If, however, you fight with a left-hander stance, the moves must be carried out laterally inverted.

Chakid practices attack combinations with the former Lumpini champion Ningsajam Fairtex. Ningsajam starts with a knee kick of the front leg, Fairtex Gym, Bangkok, 2000.

# Chapter 2
# Sequence of Combinations

**Combination of Two Techniques**

1. Jab (l), rotating elbow (r)
2. Jab (l), straight knee kick (r)
3. Straight rear punch (r), round kick (r)
4. Side hook (l), leg kick (r)
5. Uppercut elbow (l), rotating elbow (r)
6. Leg kick (l), straight rear punch (r)—see also sequence of photos
7. Round kick to the body (l), straight front kick to the head (r)
8. Straight front kick (l), jab (l)
9. Straight front kick (l), round kick (r)
10. Straight knee kick (l), rotating elbow (r)—see also sequence of photos

### Suggestion 6:

The combination of leg kick and straight rear punch. From the starting position you deliver a kick to the opponent's inside thigh. You follow it up with a straight punch from the rear. In training, kicks to the leg may only be suggested. As an alternative the trainer could wear shin guards and could then block kicks delivered at medium strength.

### Suggestion 10:

The combination of straight knee kick and rotating elbow. From the starting position you deliver a straight knee kick with the front leg. You promptly follow up with a rotating elbow, for which you use the rear arm.

## Combination of Three Techniques

1. Jab (l), straight rear punch (r), jab (l)

2. Jab (l), straight rear punch (r), rotating elbow (r)—

   see also sequence of photos

3. Jab (l), side hook (r), uppercut elbow (l)

4. Side hook (l), uppercut elbow (r), side elbow (l)

5. Leg kick (l), round kick to the head (l), straight rear punch (r)

6. Round kick to the body (l), jab (l), straight knee kick (r)

7. Round kick (r), side hook (r), uppercut elbow (l)

8. Straight front kick (l), jab (l), leg kick (r)—

   see also sequence of photos

9. Straight front kick (l), straight knee kick from a distance (r), rotating elbow (r)

10. Straight front kick (r), round kick to the body (l), round kick to the head (r)

## Suggestion 2:

The combination of jab, straight rear punch, and rotating elbow. From the starting position you deliver a jab. This is followed up by a straight punch from the rear and ends with a rotating elbow.

## Suggestion 8:

The combination of straight front kick, jab, and leg kick. Carry out a forward kick with the front leg to the opponent's body. When returning the leg to the floor you deliver a jab. Subsequently, follow up with a kick to the outer thigh of the opponent's rear leg.

The photos show trainer Oliver Glatow and the author at the Rangsit Stadium, Bangkok, 2000. Once a week Thai TV presents live coverage of fights from this ring.

## Combination of Four Techniques

1. Jab (l), straight rear punch (r), knee kick (l), uppercut elbow (r)—see also sequence of photos
2. Jab (l), straight rear punch (r), round kick (r), straight front kick (l)
3. Jab (l), straight knee kick (r), clinch grip, knee kicks in a clinch (l) + (r)
4. Leg kick (l), round kick to the head (l), straight rear punch (r), round kick to the body (r)—see also sequence of photos
5. Round kick to the body (l), jab (l), straight rear punch (r), round kick to the head (r)
6. Round kick (r), straight rear punch (r), straight knee kick (r), rotating elbow (r)
7. Straight front kick (l), straight rear punch (r), straight knee kick from a distance (r), elbow from above (r)
8. Straight front kick (l), straight knee kick from a distance (l), side hook (r), uppercut elbow (l)
9. Straight front kick (r), leg kick (l), round kick (l), straight knee kick from a distance (l)
10. Side kick (l), jab (l), straight rear punch (r), straight knee kick from a distance (r)

## Suggestion 1:

The combination of jab, straight rear punch, knee kick, and upper-cut elbow. From the starting position you start with a jab, after which you use a straight punch from the rear. You follow this up with a straight knee kick from the front leg and finally conclude the combination with an uppercut elbow.

### Suggestion 4:

The combination of leg kick, round kick to the head, straight rear punch, and round kick to the body. Start the combination with a kick to the opponent's thigh. (In training, kicks to the legs may only be suggested, in order to avoid injury to the pad holder.) This is followed by a hard kick to the head. Subsequently, you deliver a straight rear punch and finally conclude the combination with a round kick to the body.

## Combination of Five Techniques

1. Jab (l), round kick to the body (r), round kick to the body (l), straight front kick (r), round kick to the head (l)

2. Jab (l), straight rear punch (r), side hook (l), clinch grip, knee kick in clinch (r), rotating elbow (r)—see also sequence of photos

3. Straight rear punch (r), round kick to the body (r), straight rear punch (r), front kick (l), elbow from above (r)

4. Side hook (l), side hook (r), uppercut (l), rotating elbow (r), spinning elbow (l)

5. Leg kick (l), round kick to the head (l), straight rear punch (r), round kick to the body (r), straight front kick (l)

6. Round kick to the head (l), leg kick (r), side hook (r), uppercut (l), straight knee kick (r)

7. Round kick to the body (l), jab (l), round kick to the body (r), followed by another round kick to the body (r), side kick to the head (l)

8. Straight front kick (r), leg kick (l), straight knee kick (r), spear elbow (r), leg kick (r)

9. Straight front kick (l), leg kick (r), round kick to the body (r), straight knee kick (l), straight punch to the stomach (r)

10. Straight front kick (r), leg kick (l), round kick to the body (l), straight front kick (l), round kick to the head (l)

The author in training at the Rangsit Stadium, Bangkok, 1999.

### Suggestion 2:

The combination of jab, straight rear punch, side hook, knee kick in clinch, and rotating elbow. From the starting position you begin with a jab and straight rear punch. After the side hook you grab the sandbag, as in clinching. You initially take a hold with the left hand. This is followed by a knee kick, and the combination is concluded with a rotating elbow.

## Part V

# Defense and Counter Techniques

The fighter leans back to avoid the opponent's kick, Lumpini Stadium, 2001.

# Chapter 1

# Introduction

Having gotten acquainted with the attacking techniques and their combinations in the previous chapters, you will now learn how to defend yourself against the techniques and how to counter. This part of the training should be taken up only after you have succeeded in correctly mastering and swiftly delivering a basic selection of attacking techniques. Always try to follow a defense with a counter; otherwise, the opponent will continue to deliver new techniques without interruption.

Generally, defense and counter techniques with the least number of implementation steps are the most likely to succeed. Some Thai boxing trainers teach techniques with many different steps. In theory, the use of such techniques is certainly possible; however, in a real fight these techniques are very rarely observed. After all, a fighter does not patiently await the conclusion of his opponent's defense and counter techniques, but will try to interrupt these at the earliest possible occasion so as to apply his own attacking techniques.

This book presents a basic repertoire of defense and counter techniques that athletes should learn and apply in a competitive situation. In the course of your athletic career you should complement the selection with additional techniques. A large number of techniques can be learned from different trainers or can be discovered in films or competition. However, each individual athlete has different physical attributes and skills, which is why some techniques are more suitable and others less suitable. Repeated practice can answer fairly quickly the question of which of the techniques is effective for you. A list of many effective defense and counter techniques against all possible attacks can be found in the book *Muay Thai: Advanced Thai Kickboxing Techniques* (Delp, 2004).

Initially select three to five techniques and practice these in the following weeks for as long as is required to arrive at a degree of perfection. After some weeks of training, start practicing the next defense and counter techniques. This way you extend your repertoire of techniques step by step and will develop into a versatile fighter who is not easily judged by his opponents. However, the techniques must be practiced time and again for perfection of the delivery and timing. This will improve your speed, power, and timing until such time that you are finally able to deliver the techniques instinctively. It does not make any sense, though, to practice a large number of defense and counter techniques for only short periods. If you do not perfect the techniques, they cannot be used successfully in a fight. The correct moment for the use of a technique may already be over by the time you start to consider using it.

Professional athletes also practice defense and counter techniques in all training sessions, thereby improving their skills. As soon as you learn about your opponent in the next fight, your trainer will develop a training program with defense and counter techniques tailored to the opponent's characteristics.

## Note

Include defense and counter techniques in all training sessions. Discuss the attacking, defense, and counter techniques with your partner in training. He attacks with the agreed technique for a few minutes, and you defend and counter as discussed. To avoid injury, do not deliver the techniques with full power. However, the techniques must be carried out correctly; otherwise, they are often not successful. The counterpunch technique, for example, will be successful only with your body stretched toward the opponent.

Subsequently, the roles change and you now attack your training partner.

# Basis for Defense

Bear in mind that in training you should never exclusively learn only one defense. The athlete must always counter after an attack; otherwise, the opponent will be able to continue the attack. The defense techniques are, therefore, taught in such a way that the athlete initially carries out the defense, after which he follows up with a counter.

Four possible defense techniques can be applied. The "faster attack" already includes the counter.

## 1. Faster Attack

Once you detect the opponent's technique, you carry out a faster technique by which you hit your target prior to the delivery of the opponent's technique. To this end, you deliver a technique either in a straight line to the front—for example, a straight punch or a front kick—or you move forward sideways, which provides you with more time for the use of your own technique—for example, a side hook.

**A:** *Christoph (left) attacks with a straight punch from the rear. Somchok defends himself with a front kick.*

## 2. Dodging

You can prevent the success of an opponent's technique by dodging—for example, by a step to the rear or leaning back. Subsequently, the opponent will be in an unfavorable position, and you carry out a counter technique.

**B:** *Somchok (right) attacks with a jab. Christoph defends himself and leans back.*

### 3. Deflection of the Opponent's Technique

Many of the opponent's techniques can be deflected to the side, such as the straight punch or the front kick. Subsequently, the opponent will be in a disadvantageous position, which leaves him open for effective counter techniques.

**C:** *Chawan (left) attacks with a side kick. Patiphan defends himself by deflecting the kick to the side.*

C

D

### 4. Block

Another possibility to prevent the success of the opponent's technique is the block. On principle, however, the other three types of defense must be preferred, as a block always has to absorb the impact. In a fight, however, many techniques come as a surprise and are very quick, particularly techniques to the head and from a close distance. The athlete, for example, may be able to protect himself against an unexpected elbow only by his arms held up as a block for defense. To ensure success of the block you must always pay attention to a raised guard, which must never be dropped in the process of techniques. Subsequently, try to counter in order to stop the opponent in his attack.

**D:** *Chawan (left) attacks with a rotating elbow. Patiphan defends himself with a block.*

Chapter 2

# Tactics to Counter Fist Attacks

## ■ 2.1 Counterpunch

| Opponent's Technique: Jab using the same stance |
| --- |

**Execution:**

Block the opponent's punch with a strong open rear hand, to which end you firmly press the thumb into the cavity at the beginning of the biceps of your front arm. At the same time, counter with a jab. Ensure that you stretch your hitting arm to the front and that you shift your weight in the opponent's direction.

**A–B:** *Somchok (right) attacks with a jab. Christoph blocks the technique and counters with a jab.*

A

B

**A**

**B**

**C**

## ■ 2.2 Lean Back and Punch

> **Opponent's Technique: Jab, straight rear punch**

### Execution:

Lean back, so that the attack misses the target. Shift your weight to the rear leg and slightly pull your chin down to the chest for protection of the larynx. After the opponent has missed his aim, he will return his arm to the starting position. In the process you lean somewhat to the front and deliver a straight punch, while shifting your weight toward the opponent.

**A–C:** *Somchok (right) attacks with a jab. Christoph slightly leans back to avoid the opponent's technique. He promptly counters with a jab.*

As an alternative, you can also take a quick step to the rear before you return with a step forward and a counter.

# ■ 2.3 Deflect and Punch

> **Opponent's Technique: Powerful jab, straight rear punch**

## Execution:

Deflect the opponent's punch with the opposite hand to the inside, while turning the upper part of your body. Promptly counter with a straight punch and turn the upper part of your body back for additional power. Keep your body relaxed and do not deflect the opponent's arm too far to the inside; otherwise, you will be unable to perform any quick moves.

**A–C:** *Somchok (right) attacks with a straight punch from the rear. Christoph deflects the technique to the inside and counters with a straight punch to the unguarded head.*

The technique can also be used against a powerful jab.

A

B

C

A

B

C

## ■ 2.4 Block Up and Knee Kick

> **Opponent's Technique: Straight rear punch**

### Execution:

Block the opponent's punch with the opposite lower arm to the top. You then use the other arm for a hold on the opponent's neck and deliver a knee kick. Keep your lower arm up, so that the opponent's body remains unguarded.

**A–C:** *Christoph (left) attacks with a straight punch from the rear. Somchok blocks the punch to the top, pulls Christoph's neck toward him, and then delivers a knee kick with the rear leg.*

As an alternative you can also deliver the front knee to the unprotected area of the body. In that case, the opponent is not held by the neck and pulled to the front, but the knee kick is carried out promptly after the block. Try both variants, and use the one easier for you.

# ■ 2.5 Uppercut Elbow

> **Opponent's Technique: Side hook, swing**

## Execution:

As soon as you detect the beginning of the technique, turn the upper part of your body sideways. At the same time, deliver an uppercut elbow with the opposite arm. In the process you must not deliver the elbow too far to the top—as is normal for an uppercut elbow—but you must shift the elbow joint from the starting position to the front. Otherwise, you are in danger of being hit. Subsequently, you can carry out a rotating elbow with the other arm.

**A–C:** *Somchok (right) attacks with a side hook. Christoph defends himself with an uppercut elbow. In the process, he does not initially drop his arm, but carries out the technique from the starting position to protect his head.*

A

B

C

A

B

C

# ■ 2.6 Block and Elbow

> **Opponent's Technique: Body hook to the ribs**

### Execution:

The opponent delivers a body hook to the ribs. Block the hook with the opposite arm. Also turn the part of your body under attack to the front, so that the hook does not make contact at full strength. You promptly follow with a rotating elbow or an uppercut elbow with the other arm.

**A–C:** *Christoph (left) attacks with a hook to the body. Somchok blocks the hook and counters with a rotating elbow.*

In training you may only suggest elbow techniques, so as to avoid injury to your partner.

## Chapter 3

# Tactics to Counter Elbow Attacks

### ■ 3.1 Block and Knee

> **Opponent's Technique: All elbow techniques from above or the side**

**Execution:**

Block the opponent's elbow technique with the opposite arm, then follow up with a straight or lateral knee kick. Keep the lower arm up, so that the opponent's body remains unprotected.

**A–C:** *Christoph (left) attacks with a rotating elbow. Somchok blocks the technique and follows up with a knee kick to the unprotected part of the body.*

A

B

C

**A**

## ■ 3.2 Block and Elbow

> **Opponent's Technique: Rotating elbow, side elbow, uppercut elbow**

### Execution:

Block the opponent's technique with the opposite arm. In the process, move your block somewhat forward, so that the attack does not hit your guard at full force. Then deliver a rotating elbow with your other arm.

**A–C:** *Patiphan (left) attacks with a rotating elbow. Chawan blocks the technique and counters with a rotating elbow.*

**B**

**C**

# ■ 3.3 Step Forward and Elbow

| Opponent's Technique: Spinning elbow |

### Execution:

As soon as the opponent starts his turn, you take a step to the front, turn your upper body to the side, and deliver an elbow to the back of his head. Deliver the elbow and move the leg forward, which is farther away at the beginning of the opponent's attack. If the opponent turns in a clockwise direction, you hit with the left elbow and move the left leg forward, and vice versa. Ensure that you shift your weight to the front. If you move your body sideways for extra distance from the opponent's attack, you will become slower and achieve little impact.

**A–C:** *Patiphan (right) attacks with an elbow technique from a clockwise rotation. Chawan defends himself with an uppercut elbow of the left arm. If Patiphan were to attack from the other side, Chawan would have to hit with the right elbow and change his stance in the process.*

If the opponent's technique makes first contact, block it with the raised arm without interruption of your own elbow technique.

A

B

C

# Chapter 4

# Tactics to Counter Kicking Attacks

## ■ 4.1 Pull the Leg Back and Kick

> **Opponent's Technique: Kick to the inside of the leg**

### Execution:

Retract your leg under attack in a semi-circle movement, so that the opponent's kick misses the target. For greater agility, perform a sweeping turn with the stretched upper part of your body. You now counter with a round kick or a knee kick, using your rear leg.

**A–C**: *Christoph (left) attacks with a kick to the inside of the leg. Somchok pulls his leg back and counters with a round kick.*

It is risky to use this technique for a kick to the outside of the leg, as the opponent may possibly hit the pivot leg.

A

B

C

**A**

**B**

**C**

**D**

# ■ 4.2 Block and Kick

> **Opponent's Technique: Kick to the outside of the leg, round kick to the body**

### Execution:

Block the opponent's kick with the opposite shinbone, while keeping the foot and the pivot leg stretched. Raise the blocking leg in accordance with the level of the opponent's kick. In the event of a kick to the body, raise your leg all the way up to the elbow. Subsequently, briefly return your foot to the floor and promptly counter with a round kick to the opponent's head or body, using the same leg.

**A–C:** *Patiphan (left) attacks with a leg kick. Chawan blocks the technique with the opposite leg, briefly steps on the floor, and, subsequently, carries out a round kick.*

The technique can also be used for a kick to the inside of the leg; however, the counter will be considerably more difficult.

**D:** *Patiphan attacks with a kick to the body, which is why Chawan raises his blocking leg up to the elbow.*

# ■ 4.3 Jab

> **Opponent's Technique: Kick to the inside of the leg, kick to the outside of the leg, round kick to the body, high round kick**

## Execution:

As soon as you notice the beginning of a kick, take a quick straight step forward and deliver a jab at the same time. In the process, shift your weight to the front and stretch your arm and body toward the opponent. The opponent then loses his balance and his kick technique will be stopped. Subsequently, depending on your distance from the opponent, you carry out further attacking techniques.

**A–C:** *Patiphan (right) attacks with a round kick to the body. Chawan defends himself by taking a step forward together with a jab.*

In training do not deliver your punch to the face. To prevent injuries, you should slightly push your opponent's chest with the palm of the hand.

A

B

C

**A**

**B**

**C**

**D**

## ■ 4.4 Front Kick

> **Opponent's Technique: Kick to the inside of the leg, kick to the outside of the leg, round kick to the body, high round kick, spinning heel kick**

### Execution:

As soon as you notice the beginning of the opponent's technique, deliver a front kick to the stomach. The opponent loses his balance, and the kick technique will be stopped. Subsequently, depending on your distance from the opponent, carry out a round kick or a knee kick.

**A–C:** *Patiphan (right) attacks with a round kick to the body. Chawan defends himself with a front kick, using the rear leg.*

The kick can be carried out with the front or rear leg. Practice both sides in training, so that the appropriate technique can instinctively be used in a fight. After a front kick with the rear leg, you return the kicking leg to the floor. You will now be able to deliver a powerful subsequent technique with the other leg.

**D:** *The technique to the back against a spinning heel kick.*

# Chapter 5

## Tactics to Counter Pushing Foot Attacks

### ■ 5.1 Step Back

| Opponent's Technique: Front kick, side kick, back kick |
|---|

**Execution:**

Protect yourself against the opponent's kick by taking a step to the rear. Additionally, stretch your upper body somewhat away. You are able to counter only if the opponent delivers his technique with power—frequently he will use the rear leg—and loses his balance when missing the target, thereby falling slightly to the front. You then deliver a round kick with the rear leg.

**A–C:** *Chawan (right) delivers a front kick to the body. Patiphan takes a step back and slightly leans his upper body away. He then counters with a round kick.*

If the opponent aims for the upper body, lean your upper body farther away. Ensure that you pull your chin toward the chest for protection of the larynx.

A powerful front or side kick to the leg is rarely used. In this case you will be able to protect yourself by taking a big step or jump to the rear, after which you can counter with a kick.

In training you must practice kick and counter techniques at different heights.

**A**

**B**

**C**

**D**

# ■ 5.2 Deflect

> **Opponent's Technique: Front kick and side kick to the body**

## Execution:

As soon as you notice the beginning of the opponent's kick, you jump or take a swift step to the outside, while not changing the distance between your feet. At the same time, deflect the kick to the side. Do not hold on to the kicking leg, but deflect it in a continuous move to the outside.

If the opponent uses the left leg, you must step to the right, and deflect the kick with the left wrist to the left. As an orthodox fighter you must change your stance. However, if the opponent uses his right leg, you must move to the left and deflect the kick with the right wrist to the right. In this case, a left-hander must change his stance.

Depending on the distance to the opponent, you counter with a straight rear punch, a knee kick, or a round kick, using the rear leg.

**A–D:** *Chawan (left) attacks with a front kick to the body. Patiphan deflects the technique to the side and takes a simultaneous step to the outside, changing his stance in the process. He then counters with a round kick.*

# Chapter 6

# Tactics to Counter Knee Attacks from a Distance

## ■ 6.1 Step to the Side and Side Hook

> **Opponent's Technique: Straight knee kick from a distance**

**Execution:**

As soon as you notice the beginning of the opponent's technique, take a step with the outside foot to the side. For a step to the right, fighters with an orthodox stance must change their stance; left-handers must change their stance for a step to the left. Simultaneously, deliver a side hook to the opponent's head. Promptly follow up and deliver a rotating elbow with the punching arm.

**A–C:** *Patiphan (right) attacks with a knee kick from a distance. Chawan defends himself by taking a step with the right leg to the right, thus changing his stance, and promptly delivers a side hook.*

A

B

C

D

**D**:  *As an alternative to the hook you can also use a straight punch to the head. In training, practice the technique by slightly pushing the partner's chest with the palm of your hand. Deliver the technique with the power required to disturb the opponent's timing.*

A

Chapter 7

# Tactics in Clinch Situations

## ■ 7.1 Half-Shin, Half-Knee Kick

**Opponent's Technique: Knee kick in a clinch situation**

**Execution:**

You can prevent the beginning of knee techniques by carrying out a half-shin, half-knee kick to the opponent's thighs. Ensure that the technique is delivered quickly; otherwise, the opponent may already have started a knee kick.

**A–C:** *Chawan has applied the inner grip and is, therefore, in a better position. Patiphan avoids the pushes and throws by delivering a half-shin, half-knee kick to the thighs.*

**D:** *If the opponent has already started a lateral knee kick, you can use a block with the opposite knee. Aim your knee toward the center of the thigh.*

**B**

**C**

**D**

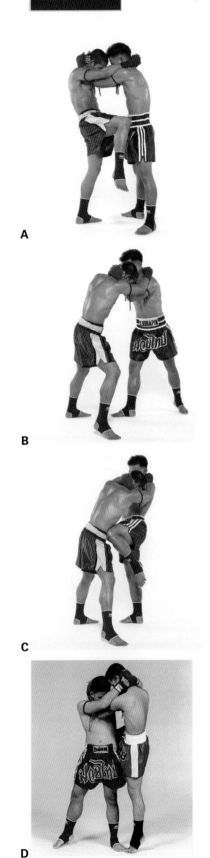

A

B

C

D

# ■ 7.2 Push to the Side

> **Opponent's Technique: Lateral knee kick in clinch situations**

## Execution:

The technique is used if the opponent carries out several lateral knee kicks in sequence. He tires in the process and will no longer be able to clinch and push with the same power, so that it will be easier to apply a throw. For protection against the knee kicks, turn your hip to the inside, thereby moving into the opponent. The thigh, and not the knee, will now hit you, and the impact will not be nearly as hard.

As soon as you notice the beginning of an opponent's knee technique, push the opponent toward the floor in the opposite direction of the kick. Subsequently, counter with a knee kick to the body.

**A–C**: *Patiphan (left) applies a lateral knee technique. Chawan notices the beginning of the technique at an early stage and pushes Patiphan toward the floor in the opposite direction of the kick. Subsequently, he carries out a knee kick.*

As an alternative you can also throw the opponent in the direction of the kick. This may result in a fall; however, it will then be difficult to use a knee technique.

**D**: *Inside turn of the hip. If the opponent kicks with the left leg, you turn to the left. If he attacks with the right leg, you turn to the right.*

# ■ 7.3 Block and Rotating Elbow

> **Opponent's Technique: Grip from below in a clinch situation**

### Execution:

The technique is used if you succeeded with an inside hold around the opponent's neck, and he now tries to rectify the situation by gripping with one hand from below. First block his hand somewhat downward, after which you deliver a rotating elbow to the unprotected part of the opponent's head. Ensure that you carry out the brief hold of the opponent's arm and the elbow technique in a continuous and swift move.

**A–C**: *Patiphan (left) attempts to gain a hold of Chawan's neck from below. Chawan defends his position by blocking the opponent's hand and subsequently delivering a rotating elbow to the unprotected area of the head.*

In training, push the arm down with power; however, the subsequent elbow technique should not be completed to avoid injury to your partner.

A

B

C

**A**

**B**

**C**

# ■ 7.4 Push Away

> **Opponent's Technique: Inside grip in a clinch situation**

## Execution:

If the opponent attempts to succeed in an inside grip, or if his grip is not firm, you can push him away. Move the palm of one hand to his chin from below, and place the other palm on top. Stretch your arms and push the opponent's chin away from you. Subsequently, you can deliver a kick or a knee kick.

**A–C:** *Patiphan (left) tries to succeed with a firm inside clinch grip. Chawan defends himself by pushing Patiphan's head to the rear.*

In training, the technique should be carried out with little power only; otherwise, it may be possible to injure the partner by overstretching his head to the back.

# Part VI

# Training

The moment before the knockout. The round kick makes contact at full strength.

# Chapter 1

# Tips for Training

Thai boxers, who thrill us with their spectacular kicks, fighting power, and stamina, had to undergo many years of hard training to reach this performance level. You can also acquire extraordinary skills provided you continually practice all elements of Muay Thai.

Muay Thai was initially taught centuries ago. Many elements of the *historical training* can also be found in today's Muay Thai training. However, the historical methods were further developed and adapted to scientific findings. This also applies to the development of the equipment—for example, boxing gloves, Thai pads, and head protection—which facilitated the improvement of training methods.

At the present time, one balanced training session comprises the following *training contents*. In shadow boxing the attacking,

This group photo was taken at the Muay Thai Institute, Bangkok, 1999.

defense, and counter techniques are practiced into the air. In sand-bag and pad training, the athlete develops timing and power for the techniques. In partner training, clinch training, and sparring he learns the application of techniques on a real individual. It is always important to cooperate with the training partner and not to inflict reciprocal injuries.

The athletic aims decide the *training plans.* Sport-specific training sessions are sufficient to learn the martial art. However, if the athlete has ambitions to compete in fights, he must plan additional training sessions for stamina and power. It must also be borne in mind that the athlete must continue to change his training to avoid stagnancy in performance.

# Chapter 2
# Historical Training

Centuries ago natural, everyday products and objects were included in training. For example, coconuts, lemons, and a Pa Kaw Ma were used. A Pa Kaw Ma is a piece of cloth, similar to a towel, which was worn around the hips instead of trousers or a belt.

The training was somewhat different from trainer to trainer. It was usually structured along the following steps:

The student was initially shown the starting position. Subsequently, he had to practice the Muay Thai steps until such time that they started to look natural and entered his subconscious mind, regardless of how long it took.

The next step was the teaching of the punch technique with the help of a Pa Kaw Ma. The student put it around his shoulders and took the ends by his fists. In this way he practiced the straight punch with a concurrent step, while holding the other hand up for protection.

Fighter Mahadeth demonstrates the training with the Pa Kaw Ma.

Two of these towels were initially used for protection of the hands in sparring. The following steps differed very much from teacher to teacher, which is why only a few of the traditional training methods will be explained.

One method to learn falling down involved the trainer having two sticks in his hands. He hit the student on one side, to which he then had to fall. This was practiced until such time that the student was able to roll off.

Fist and elbow technique training with a coconut in the water.

Training on a banana tree.

The muscles were trained on a coconut tree. The student had to climb up by holding on to the tree with his stretched arms. In this way he developed his arm, shoulder, back, and leg muscles.

Lemons were also used for training. They were attached neck-high to pieces of string. The student moved along the row of lemons delivering punches, elbow techniques, and defense and counter techniques. This training method taught timing and vision. The trainer was thus in a position to ascertain whether his student was instinctively able to defend himself correctly.

Swimming and jogging knee-high were done in the ocean and in lakes and rivers. Another training method was for the student to practice punches and elbow techniques with the water at chest level and to hit the water from above. In the process, he tried to avoid blinking and practiced defense techniques against the splashing water. He also put a coconut into the water and followed it with punches and elbow techniques, until holes appeared in the nut, water flowed in, and it eventually went down. This was initially practiced with bandaged hands, while advanced students used their bare hands.

A banana tree was chopped head high and put into the sand. The student had to punch, push, and kick the tree from different sides until it broke.

# Chapter 3
# Training Contents

The training phases include "warm-up," "main section," and "cool-down." In the warm-up phase you must prepare your body for the training. You carry out some exercises to warm up your body, after which you stretch your muscles.

In the main section of the training you study some of the basic techniques and combinations and practice these in shadow boxing. Subsequently, you must practice your skills swiftly and with power on the sandbag. This is followed up with training using the pads and with a partner. Advanced students also practice with a sparring partner.

The third phase of training usually commences with some muscle strengthening exercises. Concentrate on the muscles in your upper body and on the muscles neglected in previous training. The training is concluded with some stretching exercises and the cooling down of the muscles. These exercises help in a quick regeneration of the body and prevent tensioning and hardening of the muscles.

The following recommended time periods are for guidance. Each trainer develops his own program. However, it must be somewhat similar to the following program, to ensure that it comprises all the important elements of the Muay Thai training.

If you practice on your own, you should adapt the following details to your own requirements and performance level. If, for example, you are aiming for greater agility, you can intensify the stretching program. Or, if you do not have a partner, extend the shadow boxing and the training on the sandbag. The muscle workout can be neglected if you regularly exercise your muscles in other training sessions. However, during each training session you must warm up, stretch, and cool down.

## Thai Boxing Hour

1.  WARM-UP

    1.1 Warm-up                           Time: 5–10 min.

    Exercises to warm up the body

    1.2 Stretching                       Time: minimum 10 min.


2.  MAIN SECTION

| | |
|---|---|
| Shadow boxing | Time: 5–15 min. |
| Sandbag training | Rounds: 3–5 |
| Pad training | Rounds: 3–5 |
| Partner training | Time: 10–15 min. |
| Sparring | Rounds: 3–10 |
| Clinch training | Time: 5–15 min. |


3.  COOL-DOWN

    3.1 Muscle workout             Time: 10–20 min.

    Strengthening of the muscles

    3.2 Cooling down               Time: approx. 5 min.

    Warm-up exercises with little intensity

    3.3 Stretching                       Time: 3–5 min.

    Slight stretching for regeneration

## Warm-up

In the warm-up phase you prepare your body for training. The initial warm-up is followed by stretching. The body becomes fitter and is less susceptible to injuries.

## Warm-up Exercise

You start with an activity that warms up your body and prepares it for training. Select an exercise that can be carried out at a constant pace. You should feel comfortable and must not overexert yourself. Avoid extreme situations and do not carry out any quick and abrupt moves. This phase is meant to prepare your body for training and not for performance. Choose a level at which you are still just able to hold a conversation. The moves should be carried out for a period of five to ten minutes, best until such time that your body produces the first drops of sweat. You will now be in the best possible shape for the stretching exercises.

Slow jogging and skipping are well suited for the warm-up. In the early phase of skipping you should not do any high or difficult skips—for example, double skips—to avoid injury. "Boxing on the spot" is also suitable for the warm-up. The exercise is carried out with the legs shoulder-width apart, and you deliver uppercuts, head-high straight punches, and straight punches high up into the air without interruption. In the process, repeatedly bend your knees somewhat, but do not leave the standing position. The exercise should last a few minutes.

## Stretching

Now that you have warmed up your body, you can start with the stretching. Stretch all your muscles, particularly the weak points. Stretching lessens the tensioning in the muscles, and the body becomes flexible. Without stretching you are in danger of injury when carrying out the techniques. The body will also not be properly prepared for the next activities and cannot produce optimum performance.

Stretch yourself as often as you like. If you notice any tension in your muscles, stretch these and feel how the tension disappears. Stretching exercises must be carried out regularly, even though you interrupt your training. After some months with many stretching exercises you will be able to perform "extreme" moves, such as high kicks.

For the stretching program you should plan a period of at least ten minutes. However, if agility is the main aim of your training session, you can extend this phase at will.

## Stretching Method

The best known form of stretching has two stretch phases: light and progressive stretching. The method received international recognition through Bob Anderson (see Anderson, 1996, pages 16–20).

In the *first stretching phase* you carefully select a position in which you feel only minor stretch tension. Maintain the position for some seconds and consciously relax the muscle. Different opinions prevail on the exact execution. The author recommends counting up to 20 seconds, while you remain in this position. Having gained more experience, you will develop your own feeling and do not have to adhere to the time period any longer.

The tension should ease somewhat after a short period of time. Even if you do not feel the tension ease, you should feel comfortable in that position and be able to relax. Should this not be the case, you must relax to a certain degree and reduce the tension.

In the *second stretching phase* the stretch position will be intensified until a new tension can be felt. The position is then maintained for 20 seconds. The extended position must also be experienced as comfortable; otherwise, it must be corrected.

At the end you carefully move away from the stretch position.

- Move your muscle slowly into a position in which you can feel light tension.
- Maintain the position for about 20 seconds (first phase).
- Extend the stretching until new tension can be felt. Maintain the position also for about 20 seconds (second phase).
- Relax your muscles carefully.

## Rules

Take a stable starting position to enable full concentration on the stretching exercise. Unsteadiness at a high stretching intensity may let you exceed the optimum position and result in injury.

Move slowly and cautiously in order to find the correct stretch position. Abrupt moves may lead to serious injuries. Subsequently, use the same caution when moving away from the stretch position.

Your performance level decides the stretch position. Do not try to take up the same stretch position as your partner in training or the individuals shown in the book. For guidance use your own feeling, as all human beings have different physical preconditions. You will also find out that the tension in your muscles will be somewhat different from day to day.

You must never attempt to reach a stretch position by force. If you feel pain, you must promptly ease the stretch position, as the muscle will continue to harden, not to relax. Your agility will improve only if you slowly accustom the relaxed muscle to the new stretch position in regular exercises.

Once you have found the correct stretch position, concentrate on the muscle to be stretched. Relax the muscle and the entire muscular system. Breathe slowly and at regular intervals during stretching, and observe the relaxation in your muscle. Extensions to the stretch position are carried out while exhaling.

Regular stretching is the prerequisite for long-term improvement and maintenance of your agility. Perform at least two stretching workouts a week and avoid lengthy breaks. A minimum of two days between stretching exercises is not a must, as the stretching in line with the above method regenerates rather than strains the body.

## Stretch Program

The following represents a stretch program that you can use when beginning Thai boxing training. Everybody can use the program, as it deals with all important muscles. In the course of time it should be adapted to your individual requirements and your improved level of performance.

However, when changing the program it must be ensured that all groups of muscles remain integrated. Each group of muscles must always be stretched separately before combining into a complex exercise. You may, for example, initially stretch the calf muscles prior to a complex exercise for the rear leg muscles. This way you avoid restrictions to the exercise intensity on account of the calf muscles.

**A:** *Stretching of the neck muscles. Lean your head to the left and lower the right arm. Placing the left hand on the head and pushing it down can intensify the stretching. Subsequently, you carry out the exercise to the right side.*

**B:** *Stretching of the neck muscles. Slowly lean your head to the front and simultaneously tense your shoulders to the back. Apply slight pressure with the palm of your hands to the back of the head to intensify the stretch.*

**C:** *Stretching of the muscles in the upper part of the back and the muscles of the outer arm, shoulder, and stomach. Join the fingers of both hands and stretch the arms forward while turning the palms away from the body and stretch your back. Subsequently, raise your arms to the top, which will automatically stretch the body.*

**D**: *Stretching of the chest and front upper arm muscles. You are in a lunge step position, arms raised in a U-shape. Push your chest forward and, at the same time, move your arms to the back until you feel a slight tension.*

**E**: *Stretching of the shoulder and upper back muscles. Move your hands crosswise in the direction of the shoulder blades. The upper arms remain in a horizontal position. Experts take a hold on the edges of the shoulder blades.*

**F**: *Stretching of the shoulder, chest, and arm muscles. The right lower arm is pointing down behind the head, which will leave the upper arm in a vertical position. Use the left hand to apply pressure to the right elbow, thereby lowering the arm.*

*Subsequently, slowly move your left lower arm behind your back from below to the top, until your hands meet. Then carry out the exercise to the other side.*

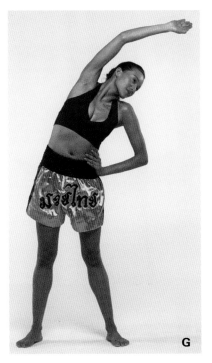

**G**: *Stretching of the lateral chest and back muscles. Stretch the right arm up into the air and lean with the upper part of your body to the left. Ensure that you stay in line with the upper body, and do not move sideways. Subsequently, carry out the exercise to the right side.*

**H**: *Stretching of the calf muscles. You are in a lunge position and the rear leg is slightly bent. Slowly stretch the rear leg and push the heel in the direction of the floor until you feel a slight tension.*

**I**: *Stretching of the muscles in the back and rear thigh. You are standing upright, the feet are close to each other, and the knees are stretched. Slowly move your upper body toward the floor.*

**J**: *Stretching of the hip-bending and the front thigh muscles. From an upright position take a hold of the foot and move it as far as possible in the direction of the buttocks until you can feel a slight tension. In the process, you must consciously move your hip forward.*

**K:** *Stretching of the rear thigh muscles, the hip-bending muscles, and the front thigh muscles. From a lunge position with the rear leg laid back, slowly push the hip and the left leg to the front until you experience a slight tension. Experts can do the splits from this position.*

**L:** *Stretching of the inner and rear thigh and back muscles. From a standing position spread your legs to the outside until you feel a slight tension. Ensure that the hip does not move away to the back. Move your upper body toward the right leg, to the center, and toward the left leg. Maintain each position for a few seconds. In the low position you move from the soles of the feet to the heels.*

**M:** *Stretching of the inner and rear thigh muscles. From a standing position with widespread legs, place your arms on the floor behind you and take a seat on the ground, while maintaining the spread leg position. Move the pelvis to the front.*

**N:** *Stretching of the inner and rear thigh and back muscles. From the previous position you stretch to the right side, to the center, and to the left side. Lean your upper body forward, as if you were pulled, and simultaneously shift your hip to the front.*

**O:** *Stretching of the muscles in the buttocks, the outside thigh, and back. Sitting on the floor with stretched legs, initially move your right leg as close as possible to the buttocks above the left leg. Push the knee with the left arm to the outside. In addition, you can bend the previously straight leg for extension of the stretch position.*

**O**

## Main Section

In the main section of Muay Thai training you learn attacking techniques, combinations, and defense and counter techniques. The session includes shadow boxing, training on sandbags and pads, and training with a partner. You must first study the techniques by shadow boxing into the air, after which you can deliver these against an object. Advanced students add sparring and clinching to their training sessions.

### Shadow Boxing

In shadow boxing the techniques and tactics are practiced into the air. Deliver the techniques swiftly, but not with full power or to completion, to protect your joints.

*Beginners* initially practice the techniques slowly, then swiftly, and, finally, in combination. The trainer closely monitors these steps, so that the athlete does not get used to mistakes. Many athletes, for example, tend to lower their guarding hand in the course of swift combinations. (When learning on your own, you can practice the techniques in front of a mirror and monitor their execution with the help of this book.)

*Advanced students* perfect their shadow boxing by acting as if they had a real opponent in front of them. They move toward him, step away, and escape to the side (see pages 49–51). In the process, they use their entire repertoire of techniques, defend themselves against the techniques of their imaginary opponent, and carry out counter attacks.

In *preparation for a fight* the shadow boxing will be tailored to the future opponent. The athlete imagines the typical style of his opponent and practices his own tactics in shadow boxing.

### Sandbag Training

In sandbag training the techniques are practiced on an object for hardening of the body, and in order to develop power and stamina in their execution. You should, therefore, try to deliver each punch, push, and kick with the greatest possible strength. However, you must ensure the correct technical execution. To avoid injuries when practicing punch techniques, you have to watch out for a straight and firm wrist.

Athletes Ningsajam and Kaew use dumbbells for more intensive training, Fairtex Gym, Bangkok, 2000.

The best-suited *training equipment* is a bag with a minimum length of 5 feet, as this will provide you with the opportunity for kicks at leg level. Untrained students initially use a bag with a soft filling—for example, cloth—as any incorrect technique entails a high risk of injury. Well-trained students use a bag with a hard filling for hardening of the shinbones. Wood shavings are a suitable filling. After some months of training a certain amount of sand can be added for hardening of the bag and to accustom the body to new requirements. The procedure can be repeated at regular intervals. However, it must be noted that only very few athletes succeed in hardening their bodies to a degree that they can practice with a bag completely filled with sand.

*Beginners* practice the combination of techniques, initially slowly and then swiftly. The trainer prescribes the combinations and monitors the athlete so that he does not develop habitual mistakes.

*Advanced students* can practice freely on a sandbag—that is, they practice without any prescribed combinations, but punch, push, and kick by instinct. The trainer watches his student and issues instructions—for example, the more frequent use of elbows—or he demands the use of certain sequences to effect changes to the athlete's fighting pattern.

Lumpini fighter Coke Fairtex in sandbag training, Fairtex Gym, Bangkok, 2000.

In *preparation for a fight* the trainer determines some combinations that are tailored to the style of the next opponent. The student must then practice these sequences time and again, so that he is able to use these instinctively in competition.

## Pad Training

In pad training the techniques are practiced on an arm-held object to develop a feeling for timing and distance. Deliver the techniques at full strength, unless the pad holder considers them to be uncomfortably hard. This may frequently happen if the trainer is consid-

Left: Apideh Sit Hiran, one of the best fighters of all time, practices elbow techniques with his student, Fairtex Gym, Bangkok, 2000.

Right: Master Decha and the author during training, Maha Sarakham Province, 1995.

erably lighter than the athlete, or if the pads are very thin. You must then practice with less power, though attention must still be paid to the correct execution of techniques.

For a *beginner* it is necessary to determine the exact technique prior to this type of training. The trainer calls the name of the technique and holds the pads accordingly. Otherwise, the risk of injury to the trainer or athlete due to an incorrect delivery will be too high. The techniques are initially carried out individually and are combined at a later stage. For perfection of the respective combination it is frequently repeated for the duration of one round (three minutes) before another combination is practiced.

*Advanced students* can carry out a free training—that is, the trainer moves the pads into a position to which the student instinctively delivers an appropriate technique. In the course of this type of training the trainer points out the athlete's mistakes. He may, for example, deliver a slight side hook with the pad to the unprotected part of the head if the athlete has dropped his guard.

Pad training is of particular importance in *preparation for a fight*, as the trainer is in a position to simulate different situations and styles. He may, for example, apply pressure to the athlete by moving toward him, demanding to be stopped by front kicks and straight knee kicks. He can also use attacking techniques for teaching counters. This way he is able to teach a fight pattern tailored to the next opponent.

## Partner Training

In partner training the attacking, defense, and counter techniques are practiced on an individual, to develop a feeling for timing and distance. The techniques will be agreed on and carried out with little power.

*Beginners* initially practice individual techniques. The technique is always announced first. The attacking athlete may, for example, deliver a jab, which the defending athlete deflects to the inside and counters with a punch. The technique is repeated for several minutes, after which the position of the attacking and the defending athlete is reversed. This is followed by the next technique. In this way the first months of training cover a basic selection of defense and counter techniques.

*Advanced students* repeat in each training session some defense and counter techniques for perfection. Furthermore, they keep on adding new techniques for extension of their repertoire. Additionally, free partner training may be chosen. In the course of this training one of the two athletes will always be attacking; the other will always defend himself and counter. It is of great importance that the attacking techniques are carried out technically correctly but with little strength; otherwise, the defending athlete may become tense and use only techniques that he masters particularly well.

In *competitive training* particular emphasis is attached to the training of defense and counter techniques by which the next opponent should be stopped. If it is known, for example, that the opponent is an aggressive fighter, special importance will be given to the training of stopping and deflection techniques.

## Sparring

Sparring is used for the free practice of attacking, defense, and counter techniques with a partner—that is, the techniques have not been agreed on beforehand. This simulates a real fight situation. Do not deliver the techniques at full strength, as this may entail the risk of injury to your partner. You must cooperate and jointly improve your performance.

Sparring may be practiced only by *advanced students*. A trainer, who will communicate mistakes, must monitor the athletes. In advance of the sparring session he will determine the body weapons to be used. Frequently, for example, only box sparring will be carried out for intensive training of the head guard. The trainer may also direct the athletes not to use their preferred techniques. In this way the athletes are forced to practice the application of other techniques and enlarge their technical repertoire for competitive fights.

For *competitive training* a partner will be selected with as many similarities to the next opponent as possible, in terms of his stature, style, and preferred techniques. The partner tries to copy the opponent's style. The athlete must then react in accordance with a fight pattern determined by his trainer.

## Clinch Training

In clinch training, gripping, holding, and the improvement of a clinch position are practiced, and knee and throw techniques are suggested. In the process, you also improve your stamina and power, particularly of the neck muscles. Strong neck muscles are of special importance to a fighter.

Clinch training, Fairtex Gym, 2000.

*Beginners* practice gripping to enter a clinch. Initially, only one hand is used for the grip; the other hand protects against the opponent's fist and elbow techniques (see pages 121–125). The athletes then practice the hold and the improvement of the clinch position, suggesting knee kicks and throws in the process. In this phase of the training, the athletes use little strength, so that they are able to concentrate on the techniques.

*Advanced students* practice the hold and the improvement of the clinch position with much strength. This is intensive training for power and stamina. However, throws and knee kicks will only be suggested to avoid injury.

In *competitive training* the hold and the improvement of the clinch position are practiced with full power. If the partner wears thick body protection, knee kicks to the body can be carried out with force; otherwise, the knee kicks will only be suggested. This type of clinching is very important and is, therefore, usually the subject of lengthy training sessions in Thai camps (10–30 minutes).

## Cool-Down

The cool-down phase in training starts with some strengthening exercises. The training is finally concluded with the cooling down of the body and some stretching exercises for the muscles.

### Muscle Workout

The following strengthening exercises are used in many gyms during the cool-down phase.

**A:** *Push-ups.* Push-ups on the fists are often carried out to improve punching power. Pay attention to a straight back when bending and stretching the arms.

**B:** *Crunch.* Raising and lowering of the upper body. The moves are not completed, so that the stomach muscles remain tense throughout the entire exercise.

**C:** *Raising the arms and legs* (Superman). From the prone position lying on the abdomen, you lift the arms, head, and legs. The final position is maintained for a number of seconds.

A

B

C

The punches to the front, from the side, or from below particularly train your chest muscles, the front shoulder muscles, and the inner rotators, which is why you should carry out some remedial exercises. You may either plan training sessions for strengthening of the muscles on Muay Thai sports-free days, or integrate some exercises into the cool-down phase of your Thai boxing training.

If you add strengthening exercises to your Muay Thai training, you should practice in accordance with the power-stamina method, which means 15–30 repetitions per set. However, using the muscle-building method with 8–10 repetitions is not recommended, as your body is already tired. Muscle build-up training should be practiced only in separate training sessions.

Strengthening exercises after the main training phase should preferably be those that strengthen the muscles of the upper back, the central and rear parts of the shoulder, and the chest.

## Cool-Down Exercises

For relaxation of the muscles you should cool down after the main training phase. This will also help in a quicker regeneration of the body. The moves should be carried out at a slow pace for approximately five to ten minutes, without physical exertion. Slow jogging or cycling at low intensity are particularly suitable cool-down exercises.

## Stretching

At the end of training you stretch the muscles once more. Do not use any extreme stretch positions, as the muscles are tired and prone to cramp. Stretch your body only in the first stretch phase and do not extend the position any farther. Stretching at the end of training serves to relax tense muscles and to prevent shortening of the muscles.

Intensive dumbbell training is recommended on days
without Thai boxing training.

# Chapter 4

# Training Plans

## Spare Time Training

Beginners first learn the basic attacking techniques and a selection of defense and counter techniques. It is necessary to practice Thai boxing at least twice a week so that progressive improvements can be made. If you practice twice a week for approximately six months, you should be able to perform the basic techniques correctly. You should gradually include more demanding techniques in your repertoire. After several years of training you will become a Muay Thai expert.

For participation in competitive fights, however, two training sessions per week will not suffice, particularly if you do not include any extra power and stamina exercises.

Muay Thai is an efficient method to get your body into shape. Photo model Tui Sang in training.

## Competitive Training at the Amateur Level

Your performance will quickly improve with three Muay Thai training sessions per week and extra fitness training. Fitness training has the effect that the improved staying power facilitates longer sport-specific training and that the techniques can be delivered with more power.

In the amateur area good results are accomplished with six training sessions per week. This can be the basis for the attainment of high competitive aims, provided you do not have to lose too much weight prior to a fight. Against this backdrop, more than six training sessions will also be required in the amateur area.

You must frequently amend your training plans for new demands to your body. If your body gets accustomed to the demands, and training becomes monotonous, your performance will stagnate. Therefore, you should determine continuously new training cycles to cover periods of 6–12 weeks, with somewhat different training aims, as shown, for example, in the 10-week cycle on the next page. After the conclusion of a cycle you practice with a slightly altered plan. It is recommended that you make notes in regard to your training plans and performance in a training diary, so that you are able to monitor the long-term development of your physical performance.

Michael Voss (athlete in the amateur world championship in Bangkok, 2003) demonstrates the flying knee kick. Trainer Ralf Kussler (www.hanuman-camp.de).

## 10-Week Cycle

The program aims to improve sport-specific performance, to which end initially the basic stamina will be developed in combination with the build-up of physical strength.

*Weeks 1–6* are planned for improvements in Muay Thai performance, for which three weekly sessions have been allocated. Additionally, the basic stamina will be improved with two sessions. You get accustomed to the power training and/or the performance level reached so far with one session per week.

The intensity of the Thai boxing training is maintained throughout *weeks 7–10*. The foremost aim in stamina training is to maintain the performance level, for which one session per week suffices. The power training is increased to two sessions per week.

|         | Day 1 | Day 2 | Day 3 | Day 4 | Day 5 | Day 6 | Day 7 |
|---------|-------|-------|-------|-------|-------|-------|-------|
| **Week 1**  | M | S | M | P | M | S | B |
| **Week 2**  | M | S | M | P | M | S | B |
| **Week 3**  | M | S | M | P | M | S | B |
| **Week 4**  | M | S | M | P | M | S | B |
| **Week 5**  | M | S | M | P | M | S | B |
| **Week 6**  | M | S | M | P | M | S | B |
| **Week 7**  | M | P | M | S | M | P | B |
| **Week 8**  | M | P | M | S | M | P | B |
| **Week 9**  | M | P | M | S | M | P | B |
| **Week 10** | M | P | M | S | M | P | B |

M = Muay Thai. The sessions are used for Muay Thai training.
S = Stamina. The sessions are used for stamina training—for example, running, cycling, or swimming.
P = Power. The sessions are used for power training. It is recommended to use a program for the entire body with dumbbells and/or power equipment.
B = Break. Training-free days for regeneration of the body.

## Competitive Training at the Professional Level

Professional athletes dedicate their entire lives to the sport for the best possible level of performance. Equal importance must be attached to correct nutrition and regeneration. One training session is usually planned for the morning, one for the afternoon. Sunday is a day of rest for regeneration of the body.

The athletes frequently prepare themselves for a fight with a 12-week training plan. Once the opponent and the framework conditions for the fight have been determined, the trainer develops a training program. The program will be tailored to the individual requirements of the athlete. It will include, for example, the weight to be shed and the opponent's style. After the fight the training intensity will be slightly reduced for regeneration of the athlete. For several weeks he will then proceed in accordance with a new cycle, by which the current performance level can be maintained and weak spots are eliminated. As soon as a new date for a fight has been determined, the trainer will develop a new competitive training program.

Fights can also be agreed to on short notice—for example, if another athlete is unable to compete and the promoter must find a replacement. Thai athletes in the lower weight divisions frequently compete in numerous fights. This requires high-intensity training throughout the year.

Thongchai Tor. Silachai. He is considered to be one of the best fighters in recent years.

## Training of Thai Professionals

In many of the Thai gyms the athletes practice in accordance with a training program that corresponds—or is very similar—to the one pictured below. The training includes six morning and six evening training sessions per week with different levels of intensity. On Sundays most of the Thai gyms are closed for regeneration of the athletes.

|  | **HARD** | **SOFT** |
|---|---|---|
| **Morning** | | |
| Running or Skipping | 4 miles / 20 minutes | 2 miles / 15 minutes |
| Shadow boxing | 15 minutes | 10 minutes |
| Sandbag training | 5 rounds | 3 rounds |
| Pad training | 5 rounds | 3 rounds |
| Partner and Clinch training | 20 minutes | 10 minutes |
| Power exercises | as agreed | as agreed |
| **Afternoon** | | |
| Skipping or Running | 20 minutes / 4 miles | 15 minutes / 2 miles |
| Shadow boxing | 15 minutes | 10 minutes |
| Sparring at high or medium intensity (three sessions per week) | 20 minutes | 10 minutes |
| Sandbag training | 5 rounds | 3 rounds |
| Pad training | 5 rounds | 3 rounds |
| Partner and Clinch training | 15 minutes | 10 minutes |
| Power exercises | as agreed | as agreed |

A completely exhausted fighter is thrown across the ropes.

# Bibliography

Anderson, Bob. *Stretching—Dehnübungen, die den Körper geschmeidig und gesund erhalten.* München, Germany: BLV Verlag, 1996.

Delp, Christoph. *Thai-Boxen basics.* Stuttgart, Germany: Pietsch Verlag, 2005.

—. *Best Stretching.* Stuttgart, Germany: Pietsch Verlag, 2005.

—. *Fitness für Männer.* Stuttgart, Germany: Pietsch Verlag, 2005.

—. *Fitness für Kampfsportler.* Stuttgart, Germany: Pietsch Verlag, 2005.

—. *Bodytraining im Fitness-Studio.* Stuttgart, Germany: Pietsch Verlag, 2004.

—. *Fitness für Frauen.* Stuttgart, Germany: Pietsch Verlag, 2004.

—. *Fit für den Strand.* Stuttgart, Germany: Pietsch Verlag, 2004.

—. *Muay Thai: Advanced Thai Kickboxing Techniques.* Berkeley, USA: Frog, 2004.

—. *Muay Thai.* Stuttgart, Germany: Pietsch Verlag, 2004.

—. *So kämpfen die Stars.* Stuttgart, Germany: Pietsch Verlag, 2003.

—. *Thai-Boxen professional.* Stuttgart, Germany: Pietsch Verlag, 2002.

—. *Bodytraining für Zuhause.* Stuttgart, Germany: Pietsch Verlag, 2002.

## Book Team

### Performers

CHAWAN DASRI
Fighter name: Chawan Sor. Vorapin
130 professional fights
Best ranking: 2nd Rajadamnern Stadium,
    also RCTI Champion
Fights in Indonesia, Japan, Korea
Manager: Peraphan Rungsikulpiphat
www.thaiboxings.com

PATIPHAN SIMALAI
Fighter name: Petchgnam Sor. Vorapin
115 professional fights
Best ranking: Challenger Rajadamnern
    Stadium, also Saraburi Champion
Fights in France, Switzerland, Japan,
    Indonesia
Manager: Peraphan Rungsikulpiphat
www.thaiboxings.com

SOMCHOK HOMKAEW
Fighter name: Chotavee Sor. Ploenjit
Approx. 100 professional fights
Approx. 60 amateur fights
Also Samrong Stadium Champion
Member of the Thai national Box Squad
Trainer: SMAC Gym, Bangkok
www.smacboxingclub.com

## Author

### CHRISTOPH DELP

Diplom-Betriebswirt (master of business administration) and author

Trainer for Muay Thai and fitness

Trainer education in Thailand from 1995 to 2001 with fight experience

Some publications: *Fitness für Männer* (2005), *Best Stretching* (2005), *Bodytraining im Fitness-Studio* (2004), *Muay Thai* (2004), *Muay Thai: Advanced Thai Kickboxing Techniques* (2004)

www.christophdelp.com

www.muaythai.de

## Photographer

### NOPPHADOL VIWATKAMOLWAT

Professional photographer since 1996 (Brooks Institute of Photography, USA)

www.astudioonline.com

## Photo Acknowledgments

Archives Christoph Delp: pages ix, 4, 6, 9, 12, 24, 28, 32, 46, 48, 53, 59, 60, 61, 119, 134, 138, 141, 143, 144, 168 (D), 169 (D), 170 (D), 175, 177, 178, 191, 192, 193, 196.

Erwin Wenzel: pages vi, 19, 20, 23, 40, 64, 132, 146, 181, 186 (F), 187 (H, J), 189, 197, 199, 202.

Songchai Ratanasuban: page 17.

Siam Sport Syndicate, Bangkok: pages v, 1, 5, 14, 26, 30, 33, 41, 43, 57, 65, 78, 89, 101, 111, 131, 145, 173, 204, 206.

Peraphan Rungsikulpiphat (Sor. Vorapin): pages 7, 10, 11.

All other photos from Nopphadol Viwatkamolwat.

**CHRISTOPH DELP** has studied intensively at many gyms and training camps in Thailand. In *Muay Thai: Advanced Thai Kickboxing Techniques,* he explains what athletes must know to succeed in actual contests. Following from the basic techniques, which the author introduces in this book, *Muay Thai Basics: Introductory Thai Boxing Techniques,* he now describes how to counter the opponent's techniques. He makes reference to well-proven attacking tactics and reviews historical Muay Thai techniques that are currently being used again by experienced fighters for surprise moves and a possible premature end of the fight.

## *About North Atlantic Books*

North Atlantic Books (NAB) is an independent, nonprofit publisher committed to a bold exploration of the relationships between mind, body, spirit, and nature. Founded in 1974, NAB aims to nurture a holistic view of the arts, sciences, humanities, and healing. To make a donation or to learn more about our books, authors, events, and newsletter, please visit www.northatlanticbooks.com.

North Atlantic Books is the publishing arm of the Society for the Study of Native Arts and Sciences, a 501(c)(3) nonprofit educational organization that promotes cross-cultural perspectives linking scientific, social, and artistic fields. To learn how you can support us, please visit our website.